Road through
the Rain Forest

ROAD THROUGH THE RAIN FOREST

Living anthropology in Highland Papua New Guinea

David M. Hayano

California State University, Northridge

WAVELAND

PRESS, INC.

Prospect Heights, Illinois

For information about this book, write or call:

Waveland Press, Inc.
P.O. Box 400
Prospect Heights, Illinois 60070
(708) 634-0081

Printed in the United States of America

7   6   5   4   3   2   1

To the memory of Irarope Ma,
storyteller and friend

Contents

Preface

I originally went to Papua New Guinea in 1969 as a postgraduate anthropology student to study agricultural change among the Awa-speakers of Tauna village. These people were suggested to me by Phil Newman, my doctoral advisor at UCLA, who had earlier conducted fieldwork in Ilakia, an Awa village a half day's walk to the south. I was accompanied by my then-wife, Jackie; together we stayed for nineteen months. The focus of my research eventually changed, as it often does, and I ended up studying the relationship between marital alliances and warfare between villages, which later formed the basis of my Ph.D. dissertation. I made shorter trips to the Awa in 1981 and 1986.

For the reader's convenience, a glossary and a list of personae are provided. Glossary terms are from Tok Pisin, the most commonly shared language throughout Papua New Guinea, and from Awa, an indigenous language spoken by approximately 1,500 people.

The term *personae* should not be misleading. These are not dramatized men and women, but actual individuals, some living, some dead, of flesh and blood. Their names have been changed and slightly altered to make their pronunciation easier for the introductory reader. Conventional ethnographies are usually writings about people with no personal names, no utterances, no feelings, no individual life experiences. Rather than beating the life out of the data, as academic writing frequently does, I have tried to squeeze it back in.

All references to money are in approximate U.S. values for the time, not Australian dollars and cents or the older pounds and shillings, both currencies of which have been replaced by the Papua New Guinea (PNG) kina and toea.

The lives that I write about—mine included (and I offer no apology for my intrusion in the text!)—are neither strictly biographical nor explained by conventional social science models. Rather, they are meant as the actual footing of data, as time-slice illustrations of a range of individual experiences that normative anthropological monographs, with their plethora of concepts applying to the aggregate, usually manage to avoid deliberately.

I gratefully acknowledge financial support for the various field trips, which were provided by a U.S. National Institute of Mental Health Pre-Doctoral Fellowship and Field Training Grant, the government of Papua New Guinea, and the Dean's Office of the School of Social and Behavioral Sciences at California State University, Northridge. The slack was taken up by my poker winnings.

Professors Bill Wormsley and Rich Scaglion read an earlier version of this manuscript, and I have benefited immensely from their insights. Tom Curtin, editor at Waveland Press, graciously and enthusiastically saw this whole project through from initial inquiry to final product. Sherri Martin, my typist, skillfully deciphered my marginalia and produced a beautiful manuscript.

My parents, Lillian Koh Hayano and the late Mieki Hayano, offered constant sustenance and encouragement through their letters and "care packages" from home.

Although my former wife accompanied me and has her story to tell, this is, ultimately, my tale of fieldwork. Jackie's activities and thoughts do not play a prominent role in this story. This is not due to oversight or lack of appreciation; in fact, the success of my fieldwork largely depended on her adaptability and companionship.

My greatest debt, which perhaps will never be paid, is to the people of Tauna village, especially Ila, Kawo, and Api, who taught me incalculable lessons about their lives and mine.

July, 1989
Ibiza, Spain

PAPUA
NEW GUINEA

PAPUA
NEW GUINEA

AUSTRALIA

5°

NEW BRITAIN

Goroka

Okapa ▲ □Awa

CORAL SEA

Port Moresby

10°

AUSTRALIA

145°

0   100   200 mi

150°

My Home

Long, long ago
before white men came,
my home was here.

My home was like a young girl
dressed in all colours.
Coconuts, bamboos, crotons
made it beautiful
where the sun shines on it,
who can describe it?

James Makain

This Wape poem is from *Words of Paradise: Poetry of Papua New Guinea* (p. 39), edited by Ulli Beier, 1973, Greensboro, NC: Unicorn Press. Reprinted with permission.

Introduction

A nthropological fieldwork is like a dream: traveling to distant places in a slightly disoriented mind and body, the observer is bombarded by a dazzling array of sensory images. Lovely, tranquil scenes must be shared with dreadful nightmares. Life and death pass before one's eyes. Emotions of every kind and depth are provoked. Unresolved contradictions and paradoxes have no trouble coexisting. But eventually all fieldwork, like dreams, must end. The weary traveler must rub his eyes and return home and begin to make sense of his experiences.

The Awa people of Papua New Guinea are subsistence horticulturalists (growing mainly sweet potatoes, yams, and taro) and pig herders who reside in the remote mountainous regions of the Eastern Highlands Province. To reach Awa country, one must walk or take a truck as far as it will go from the Okapa District office, the seat of local government, to the end of a usually muddy, vehicular road. The terminus is gradual. Tall, sharp kunai grass slowly creeps over the tire treadmarks and finally engulfs them completely. The obliterated road ends gracefully and reluctantly at a bushy cul-de-sac, the beginning of an expansive, perpetually damp rain forest, usually shrouded in a gossamer mist. From there, several narrow trails zigzag up and down steep mountain slopes, across chest-high grasslands, and through treacherous, biting rivers.

In the hilly village of Tauna, cloistered by the solid green backbone of ancient mountains, the inhabitants built us a bamboo-and-grass house in a small cleared hamlet. This was the first time either Jackie or I had lived with no electricity, no running water, no nearby stores or restaurants, and no neighbors who spoke our language. We tried to adapt to what was for us the fundamentally different rhythm of life catapulted forward and backward by different individuals and what they did. Sometimes the pace was languorous, other times frenetic; but it was always, for us, different.

This book is a narrative of fieldwork. It attempts to provide a personal and humanistic glimpse of contemporary village life in Papua New Guinea. The events are described as in a diary, in the order in which they unfolded. This is a crucial point in understanding the natural ebb and flow of activities; for too often the order of fieldwork, the living and learning, are jumbled up or completely disregarded when it is finally written up back home. Rearranging these patterns despoils others' orders of existence, for we tend to forget how desultory human lives really are. And unfortunately, anthropology does not yet have a language to adequately convey these diverse rhythms and patterns.

It is further unfortunate that social science theories of culture change for the most part tend to lack an adequate grounding in down-to-earth events. This grounding is particularly important in small-scale societies such as those of rural Papua New Guinea. Much of what happened to the Awa, how they have changed and what has changed, can only be understood by reference to the will of specific individuals.

No actual physical track of crushed stone and dirt of the kind that winds through the less mountainous areas of the north and west reach the Awa yet. To them, however, the road remains a metaphor for culture change and "development." Men talk about it feverishly and insistently point to the high rain forest where it will eventually come. The road-to-be is a symbol of salvation, of endless economic gain, a path toward material wealth and increasingly accessible consumerism.

But not all of the villagers find this talk comforting. Some are quite content with traditional village life and look at their future with more caution. Still others, mainly of the older generation, know that a road will be their final death cry. They could already see the end coming in the past several decades of contact with the uninvited arrival of pale, gum-booted Australian *kiaps* (patrol officers), Western currency, trade stores, and wage labor migration that carried their young sons on airplanes to the coastal plantations that they themselves would never see.

Sooner or later—it is difficult to say precisely when—a vehicular road, bouncing with sputtering government and commercial pickup trucks, will be built. It will link the Awa over a crude feeder track to the Okapa station, and then on to the larger towns along the Highlands Highway. When that day comes, the Awa will have to live with one less metaphor and one less dream.

Personae

Males

Abaka	A middle-aged, married, former coastal worker.
Abate	An elderly former councillor from Tawaina village.
Aborate	The young son of Nenanio.
Ante	A North Fore man.
Anto	A middle-aged, married man, thought to be crazy.
Api	The number one traditional political leader, Big Man, of Tauna village.
Awe	A young, unmarried former coastal worker.
Entobu	An elderly Big Man.
Ila	The village committeeman and a former coastal worker; my key informant.
Kawo	The village councillor and a former coastal worker.
Kawona	An Auyana man.
Kaye	A young, unmarried former coastal worker; son of Api.
Kiato	A middle-aged, married man from Kawaina village.
Kino	A young, married former coastal worker.
Kirante	Kawo's married elder brother; a plantation worker.
Konato	A middle-aged, married former coastal worker.
Konoi	A Big Man; Kawo's father-in-law.
Kuino	A young, married former coastal worker.
Mapika	A young, married plantation worker.
Matam	A young, married former coastal worker; Ila's sister's husband.
Matime	The son of Ila and Ruo.
Menua	A young, married former coastal worker; Ila's brother-in-law.
Mone	A teenage boy.

3

Nabete	The teenage son of Tintau.
Nonaka	A young, married plantation worker.
Onka	A young, married man and former coastal worker.
Panuma	A young, married former coastal worker; son of Entobu, a Big Man.
Pauwe	A middle-aged, married Big Man and former coastal worker.
Poke	A middle-aged, married man.
Puwate	A middle-aged, married man.
Sotai	An elderly Big Man.
Tati	A middle-aged, married man; the former *luluai* (government-appointed head man) of the village, before elected *kaunsil* (councillors) and *komiti* (committeemen).
Tenta	A young, married former coastal worker.
Tewe	David, the anthropologist.
Tia	Ila's teenage brother.
Tintau	A Big Man; the father of Tutu, Ruo, and Nabete; Ila's father-in-law.
Toa	A teenage boy.
Tobi	Kawo's younger brother.
Tunumu	A middle-aged, married man.
Tutu	A young, married former coastal worker; the eldest son of Tintau.
Waka	A middle-aged, married former coastal worker.
Wamani	A Big Man.
Wanu	A young, unmarried plantation worker.
Wenamo	A young man; the younger brother of Puwate.
Wepala	A Big Man.
Yagai	A policeman from Okapa.

Females

Aisara	A young, unmarried mother; later married to Kawo and then to Tenta.
Ayato	The wife of Tati; mother of five.
Ausi	Young daughter of Nenanio.
Jackie	Wife of Tewe.
Kaera	Middle-aged wife of Pauwe.
Ketawa	Ila's younger sister; the wife of Matam.
Kuintawe	A young girl; daughter of Tomo.
Kukawo	Kuino's wife; a young mother of two.
Nenanio	Middle-aged mother of five; married to a plantation worker.
Numia	A young married woman; wife of Kino.
Nunuma	Tenta's young, childless wife.
Ruo	The daughter of Tintau; Ila's wife.
So	A young Kawaina woman; wife of Wenamo.

Tai	Wife of Api.
Taiya	The wife of Anto.
Tatiti	A teenage girl.
Teara	The aged mother of Kuino.
Tewaka	Kawo's young first wife; the daughter of Konoi.
Tiara	An aged, widowed woman.
Tipia	A young, marriageable girl.
Tomo	The wife of Kirante and mother of four; later Kawo's wife.
Wetape	The young bride of Onka.
Yosepe	The young daughter of Tunumu.

Chapter 1

Dangerous Men

Bleary-eyed and travel-weary, Jackie and I finally touched down at Port Moresby, the coastal capital city of Papua New Guinea, after brief stopovers in Hawaii, Fiji, and Australia. It was the middle of January and the height of the rainy season in the Melanesian tropics. I was a graduate student in cultural anthropology at the University of California, Los Angeles, and had come to the Highlands region of Papua New Guinea to conduct my doctoral study. I had read many books on the peoples and their cultures, some of which were greatly inaccurate and sensationalized in their vivid descriptions of such apparently exotic practices as cannibalism, headhunting, warfare, and sorcery. These reports, of course, hid the immense diversity of the country and almost completely neglected to mention how rapidly everything was changing. Nevertheless, I was fueled with a desire to live among a people who were as different from me as possible.

My romantic vision of Papua New Guinea, however, was blurred at Port Moresby's Jackson Airport by the overbearing realities of the high temperature and humidity coupled with jet lag. I wore a long-sleeved shirt and jacket and discovered quite quickly that I was way overdressed for the tropics. Perspiration rolled down by forehead and arms. Struggling to collect our baggage amidst a colorful collection of fellow travelers — urban Papuan students, Highlands tribesmen, busy Australian govern-ment officials, and Asian businessmen — we were approached by a Chinese man, a resident of Rabaul on the island of New Ireland, north of the mainland. He was dressed in what was the standard costume for the country: a short-sleeved shirt, a pair of shorts, and knee socks with leather shoes.

7

"Are you Chinese?" he asked curiously, immediately trying to categorize a stranger out of place. "No, I replied. "I'm an American of Japanese ancestry."

"What are you doing in New Guinea?" he continued.

"Well, I'm an anthropology student, and I hope to study the people of a remote village in the Highlands."

"Oh, I see," he said, nodding to himself in quiet confirmation.

Since we knew nothing about the town and its facilities, our new friend, Mr. Chung, insisted on driving us closer to the city, to the Davara Motel on Ela Beach Road. Except for the unbearable high heat and humidity, it could have been a resort motel along the coast of California.

Before Papua New Guinea's independence from Australia in 1975, Port Moresby was a typical South Seas colonial creation, a socially and racially stratified city shaped by the legacies of the British, Germans, and finally the Australians. Its physical features resembled those of many other Pacific port towns: clean white houses partitioned by well-kept front yards and flower gardens where the Europeans and indigenous elite lived; a dusty merchant section of town harboring Chinese-owned shops; and, on the outskirts, sprawling shanty houses and squatter settlements, home for the many local and transient indigenes who flocked to the city in search of work.

The stifling heat of the motel room persuaded us to walk into town and purchase some supplies. Heeding the advice of other anthropologists, we stocked up on some more medicine, especially Chloroquin, malaria suppressant tablets. (This did not prevent us from eventually contracting the illness.) We walked back to the motel in the late afternoon. The temperature had not fallen one degree. The local radio station blared with the Beatles' "Day Tripper." That was followed by the world news in Tok Pisin, one of the most important languages in a country where there were known to be at least 700 different tribal tongues, some spoken by distant villagers who had never even heard of Port Moresby. The contrasts of this country were startling, difficult to comprehend. And we had only been there a few hours.

The next day we ravaged the smorgasbord lunch in the motel dining room, gobbling down as much as we could in the hope of saving my limited grant money by not eating dinner. Again, as two obvious strangers out of place who appeared to have never eaten, we attracted the attention of another observer—the hotel cook.

"Well, what do we have here? You two don't live here, in this bloody country, do you?" He continued without encouragement.

"Me, I'm a Kiwi—you know, from New Zealand. I thought I'd do some traveling around and see a bit of Australia and New Guinea before I settled down. But I can't wait to get out of this bloody place. There's nothing to do. Absolutely nothing, except drink yourself stiff. And no women!"

Walter was a friendly, large-framed skier who longed for his homeland and some new company. He took an instant liking to Jackie when he discovered that she was English. After being satiated with lunch, we took up his offer to drive us around Port Moresby to see the sights. Climbing up a winding road overlooking the bay, he excitedly pointed out the hull of a Japanese ship that had been sunk during war World War II. It stuck out of the water like a rusted cathedral. Walter gleefully recounted the fierce battle scenes between the Australian and New Zealand (ANZAC) forces and the Japanese, who had tried to capture Port Moresby during the war.

Perversely enjoying each other's incongruity, which only lonely travelers seem to relish, we made further plans to meet that evening. "Dinner," Walter reminded us, "will be in a very *exclusive* club in Port Moresby." Already uncomfortable with the racial barriers in this colonial city, but not wanting to be unfriendly to our gregarious host, we accepted.

The exclusive club was reserved for expatriate ex-servicemen of the Australian army. Many of the men, in their fifties and sixties, reveled in war stories and military celebrations and had had firsthand experience fighting the Japanese. When our strange trio entered the club, Walter towering almost a foot taller than both of us, the chattering and beer drinking palled as all heads turned toward us (or was it just me?). We hastily signed the guest register and were led to the back of the club to a table usually reserved for the Papuan busboys. Actually it was a relief to be out of staring range. Oblivious to this attention, or lack of it, Walter was his usual jovial self.

The following day we met Walter after lunch again and listened patiently to his complaints of homesickness. This time we drove for a drink to the also-exclusive Royal Papua Yacht Club. In the spacious dining area we were deferentially served iced drinks by barefoot Papuan men (addressed in Tok Pisin as *bois*), who were properly bedecked in white shirts, bow ties, and black wraparound *laplaps*. They wore no shoes. They were perfect models of colonial servitude. A host of "thank yous" and "yes sirs" followed our orders.

From the large bay windows of the Yacht Club, I could see the outlines of a shabby village. It consisted of a string of rotting, filthy shacks supported on stilts hugging the coastline. The comparative wealth of the Yacht Club made this view a totally depressing colonial nightmare.

Koki market, an open-air area near the beach, where foodstuffs are displayed on open tables or on the ground, was our next stop. I looked around and saw no Europeans there. Walter disgustedly pointed out bundles of unrecognizable fly-covered carcasses. "That's dog meat! That's cat meat! That's what they eat!" Just off the sandy beach, as if to corroborate his low opinion, several men openly relieved themselves in the sea.

Fortunately, I thought, we would be able to leave Port Moresby the next day and resume our travel to the Highlands. The city was fascinating, but our eventual destination lay far ahead of us.

The bumpy flight from Port Moresby to the Highlands gives a dramatic view of the interior of the country. From the air the landscape below consists of miles and miles of dense forest, broken only by winding rivers crawling through the bush like giant, twisting snakes. Every now and then, one can see bits and pieces of human settlements and gardens, swatches of brown against the green background.

Following a brief stopover at the east-coast city of Lae, we landed in Goroka, the administrative center of the Eastern Highlands District (now called the Eastern Highlands Province).

Drawn to the glitter of gold, European prospectors gradually made their way up from Lae and the Markham Valley to the Highlands during the 1930s. At that time, most of the Highlands were unexplored; the extent of the Highlands population was unknown. On foot, patrol officers, explorers, prospectors, and missionaries began to survey the numerous hidden mountain valleys. The rugged terrain and the recalcitrant people, settled into their own way of life, made the going difficult. But what they found were numerous local villages dotted throughout the hills and valleys. All of the people seemed to subsist on root crop cultivation, tend domestic pigs, and live in compact, palisaded villages of several hundred people. Village leaders, known as *Big Men*, gained their power through personal contact and oratory skills; they were unlike the Polynesian chiefs who ascended to authority genealogically. Mutual hostility in the forms of warfare and sorcery kept neighboring villages apart. Elaborate gift-exchange ceremonies and shared rituals occasionally brought them together in a state of temporary and shifting alliances. From valley to valley, dialect and language differences grew further apart.

The intrusive European settlers, bringing with them steel tools and cowrie shells (the latter a form of Highlands wealth before the introduction of money), gradually settled into various controlled pockets. Pacification, however, did not come easy. Casualties from rifle bullets or barbed arrows were inflicted on both sides.

Goroka is a beautiful town that rests in a mile-high, flat valley. Unlike the coast, its climate is cool and much less humid. Stores, supermarkets, banks, a pharmacy, and government offices are clustered along the main street, where both Europeans and locals do their business. When we arrived, Goroka and the entire Highlands were undergoing a period of rapid economic growth brought on by coffee, the new gold of the fertile mountain valleys.

We checked into the bungalows at the Goroka Hotel, where the manager, an old New Guinea hand, promised to show us around town. The next day he introduced us to James Sinclair, the district commissioner (D.C.)

of the Eastern Highlands. A visibly sturdy, stalwart man, Sinclair was a veteran of dozens of early patrols into the interior of new Guinea to areas on the map marked "unknown" and "unexplored."

He glanced at a letter of introduction I had sent him weeks beforehand. With official abruptness he cleared his throat and said, "The area you plan to settle in, the Awa, is administered by Mr. Peter Broadhurst of the Okapa Subdistrict office. You will have to go there and meet him in person. Good luck on your study." I took the end of that statement to mean our meeting was over.

After purchasing camping gear, supplies, and food, we set out in a rented truck with a hired driver toward the small township of Kainantu to the east, our last planned link before reaching Okapa. The Kainantu, the only hotel in town, was empty except for the bar. There we met two expatriate Australians, Ken, a local coffee buyer, and his friend, Ralph, who operated a small trade store in Okapa.

I told them of our plans. "Well, you're in luck," Ken said. "I happen to be leaving this afternoon for Okapa in my car. You can come with me, but you'd better get your gear together fast. We'll have to leave before it rains."

After what we thought would be our final drink and visit to a bar for two years, we organized our luggage, loaded it into his car, and set out on the winding dirt and rock road toward Okapa, which lay forty miles south and several thousand feet higher. But we had not left early enough to beat the rain. The sky, noisy and splendidly fulgurant, gave us a wet welcome. Every hundred yards the heavily laden car coughed to a halt, the tires spinning uselessly, wildly in the mud. Fortunately, the Fore people, the villagers whose thatch huts lined the road, helped us every bit of the way. Accustomed only to the sounds of birds, insects, rain, and other human voices, they usually came out into the open on hearing the roar of an engine. Standing in their doorways or under banana trees, they found their curiosity unwasted: what they saw was an incongruous duo of foreign "mud men" attempting to push life into a reluctant jalopy.

After three hours of pushing and puttering, we finally arrived at Ken's house, tired, wet, and discouraged. Ken lived in a magnificent, two-story house several miles outside Okapa, among the North Fore people. Although its architecture was European, its materials were local bamboo and stiff *pitpit* grass. We decided to recuperate at the house for several days in order to adjust to the cool, damp weather and the mountains until Ken returned from a coffee-buying expedition in the Gimi area to the west. I took stock of our situation so far. Somewhere between Port Moresby and Ken's house, some of our supplies had disappeared; the metal cargo boxes we ordered to be air freighted from Steamships Sheet Metal factory in Port Moresby had not yet arrived; our cash was dwindling rapidly; and to make things worse, it seemed to be the heaviest period of the rainy season.

Yet, undaunted in our plan to forge deeper into the bush, eventually toward Awa territory, we thought it to be necessary to walk as much as possible for our own future survival. But it was difficult to saunter around casually away from the dirt road. The land around Ken's house consisted of dense, massive trees, wild brush, and sharp *kunai* grass, all of which blanketed the sloping hills. The tangled undergrowth, fed by the interminable rain, was thick and wet. In Los Angeles, I had practiced walking up to the Griffith Observatory, but it was not quite the same here. At a mile-high elevation, I lost my breath much sooner than I was used to doing; and my feet, encumbered with thick, rubbery jungle boots, slipped at each step on the muddy mountain floor.

In the morning, with Ken gone, we were joined by Ante, his household helper, who took on the task of looking out for us. Since I had studied the rudiments of Tok Pisin in Los Angeles, it was possible for me to communicate, although haltingly, with him through a series of abrupt two-word sentences and dramatic gestures. Ante and I talked, and I stumbled, physically and verbally, for nearly two hours to a nearby trade store.

By the time we returned to Ken's house, the news had spread out to the surrounding villages that two foreigners from America were "practicing" walking along the roads. Just as we were preparing a tin of corned beef over a kerosene stove, the local government councillor of the North Fore stepped inside the house to pay us a visit. Since he was the local political representative for all the villagers in the census division, he had to know what was going on and what we were doing there. He was shoeless and dressed, like most men we had seen, in a pair of shorts and a short-sleeved shirt. He carried an umbrella over his shoulder and sat down to light a cigarette.

"Why do you come here?" he asked bluntly.

"Well, we won't be here long. Actually we'll be going to live among the Awa, the people who live in the hills to the southeast," I responded. "I am here to learn about their culture and language."

"No! No! You can't go there," he insisted, louder and more animated by the second. "The mountains are too steep, like climbing a tree. And the people are wild and mean. It is better to stay here. We will build you a nice house and a garden. You will be comfortable, and my people will take good care of you." He fixed his stare on me.

"But our plans are already made. I would like to, but . . ."

"It is better here," he interrupted. "I am telling you the truth. I am not a liar. This is not just talk."

After a slight pause he added, "But if you can't live here, at least you can buy some of these." Around his neck he fingered what looked like an old bead necklace. The "beads" were old German New Guinea coins with holes through the center.

"These are valuable. You need them, and I will sell them to you for a good price."

I sat there confused. What did he really want from me? "No. I can't buy them now. I am not rich," I apologized rather pathetically, and turned out the pocket of my trousers in a grand symbolic gesture to show that they were empty.

"Maski! Never mind! It was nothing. Our talk was nothing," he said. In a puff of smoke he rose and quickly left the house.

I knew by now that our petty annoyances so far were nothing. In the ensuing months of fieldwork I would also be fighting a battle of wits and power.

The next morning we packed eagerly, anticipating Ken's return. We sat in front of the house and kept an eye on the ominous dark clouds floating in over the hills. Rain, as we learned, would almost certainly mean delay. Several teenage boys walked up to us to get a closer look.

"Do you know the Awa people who live in the hills over there?" I asked.

"We do not know those people well, but we have heard that they are stubborn and dangerous," one boy said. "Walking there will make your stomach weak," another boy volunteered. I began to wonder seriously about these Fore depictions of the Awa. Was there a conspiracy to scare me and keep me here? Or was it the truth?

"Stay here. We will build you a nice house like Master Ken's and a sweet potato garden," they chimed in.

If my field site had not already been agreed upon in Los Angeles, I might have accepted their invitation. The thought of climbing even higher mountains in the middle of the rainy season did little to lift my enthusiasm or soothe my painful legs. Neither did the idea of trying to live with a bunch of "dangerous" people.

By noon the following day Ken had not yet shown up, and Jackie, Ante, and I attempted another practice walk. This time we set off in the direction of Okapa, Ante and the three teenage boys trailing along patiently. An hour's practice run was enough, we thought, and on the way back to the house our companions suggested taking a shortcut. Their shortcut meant trudging through dense undergrowth, up muddy mountain trails with no visible footpath, and over slippery felled logs balanced precariously above the streams. They were never out of breath, I observed enviously, and seemed to treat this hike as a leisurely afternoon stroll. When we approached the house, we were exhausted, and again I thought seriously about changing field sites because of the immense difficulty of walking and the worry about the load of cargo we had bought. How would we ever make it to the Awa? Who would have the strength to carry our goods in?

By late afternoon, the now-predictable dark rain clouds began to roll in, completely obliterating the remaining sunlight. There was no word of Ken. In the spare bedroom, his two inefficient kerosene lamps flickered hypnotically, and under the darkened sky Jackie and I soon fell into exhausted sleep.

By sunrise, expecting Ken to arrive at any moment, we packed up all of our gear and waited. Ante strolled by, carrying the morning water. "Where's Ken?" I asked impatiently. I was beginning to get tired of the same question.

"Master Ken is buying coffee from the Gimi people . . ."

"I already know that," I interrupted. "What is taking him so long? He was only supposed to be gone one day." I raised my index finger and repeated in Pisin, "Wan de. Wan de."

Ante, obviously, was used to these delays. "The roads in the Gimi," he reported matter-of-factly, "are completely buggered up. They're worse than they are here." It was no use asking any more questions.

Having nothing to eat, the three of us walked down the road to a small trade store and bought some tins of corned beef and a boiled chicken. Several young girls of a nearby village trailed us, giggling and screaming. Most wore only their short bark skirts. For warmth, they wrapped their arms around their shoulders, hugging themselves.

By evening, it was apparent that Ken wouldn't return. The next day, all day, we waited again, taking short walks and entertaining the children. Then nightfall. Sleeping came easy. But next, as if in a dream, I heard voices from downstairs.

"Are you two alright? Has Ante been looking out for you?" I searched for my flashlight and quickly jumped out of my sleeping bag to meet Ken coming up the stairs.

"My bloody truck was stuck in the Gimi roads," he said apologetically. "But tomorrow—for sure—I'll drive you into Okapa. Not to worry. That's the way things work in New Guinea. You'll have to get used to it. You'll learn."

My anxiety rose.

"Hope you've been sleeping well. See you in the morning." I would have to see it to believe it, I reminded myself.

At the Okapa District office, as promised, we met Peter Broadhurst, the assistant district commissioner (A.D.C.) and his gracious wife, Helen, who treated us to a sumptuous home-cooked lunch. In addition to the Broadhursts, the Okapa station included several "European" (that is, white) *kiaps* (patrol officers), a half-dozen indigenous policemen, and several office clerks. Ken's friend, Ralph, ran one of the three small trade stores. Apart from the few new Western-style houses and the office, which were built only within the last twenty years, the entire area was surrounded by traditional grass and bamboo circular Fore huts.

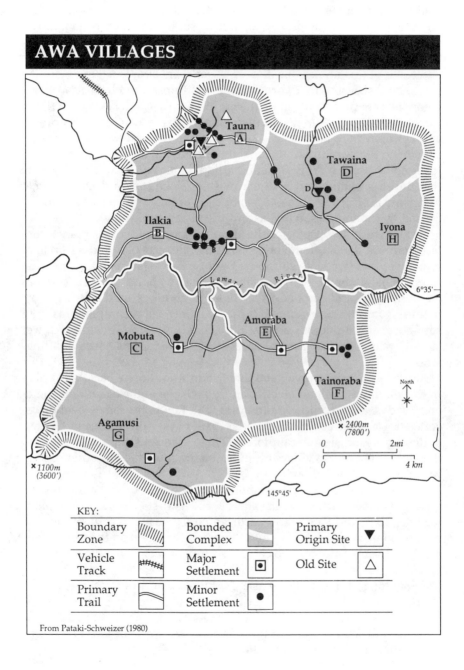

AWA VILLAGES

KEY:

Boundary Zone	Bounded Complex	Primary Origin Site ▼
Vehicle Track	Major Settlement ◉	Old Site △
Primary Trail	Minor Settlement ●	

From Pataki-Schweizer (1980)

In the early 1950s, medical science discovered that the Fore, unlike any other group of people in the world, suffered from a degenerative nervous disease known as kuru (meaning trembling or shaking). Dr. Carleton Gajdusek set up a small medical post to study the distribution and cause of this mysterious disease. After years of painstaking medical study, he discovered that kuru disease was transmitted by a slow virus when the Fore practiced cannibalism. (In 1976, Dr. Gajdusek received the Nobel Prize in physiology and medicine for his research.) Fore women and children were particularly susceptible to the disease because they consumed the partially or uncooked brains of the dead. The virus they ingested eventually debilitated and killed them. I understood, however, that the Awa people had no such disease, since they did not practice cannibalism. But they greatly feared the Fore and believed kuru to be caused by malicious sorcery, as did the Fore themselves.

Finally ready to set out for the Awa, we took stock of our cargo one last time. We had stuffed clothes, writing paper, books, and a portable typewriter into two large suitcases. With twine we fastened together the sleeping bags, chairs, two card tables, and two chaise lounges to sleep on. A dozen cardboard boxes held more supplies and tins of food, including mutton curry, cheese, a precious bottle of Australian Riesling, soy sauce, and numerous spices. But according to the Broadhursts, we lacked two of the most essential necessities: medicine and house-building tools.

At the last moment we agreed that Jackie would drive back to Goroka in the afternoon with an electrician from Okapa and stock up on some more goods. Meanwhile I would travel with Ken in his four-wheel-drive coffee truck to the end of a vehicular road, to the Fore village of Okasa, which lay near a sizable rain forest. There I would sleep the night and then hike into the Awa village of Tauna, our eventual field location. Jackie would walk in the following day.

Ken and I arrived at Okasa hamlet, just a dozen or so bamboo-and-grass huts in a clearing, by late afternoon. His first task was to summon together all of the Fore who had dried coffee beans to sell. While the men lined up with a bag here and there to be weighed on the truck, Ken assigned twenty volunteers to carry my supplies into Tauna the following morning.

"How long is the walk?" I asked a husky man in torn shorts and a T-shirt who appeared to be their most enthusiastic representative.

"Tauna is close," he said. "But it depends on the rain. If there is no rain the walk will be easy. If the rain is heavy we will have to wait in our shelters by the river until the water is low."

I nodded hesitantly.

Over my right shoulder he pointed to the grayish-green hills in the distance. "That is the way we will walk," he said. The distant mountains looked absolutely beautiful and silent, but treacherous, and I felt a sigh within me.

Ken and I wolfed down a quick dinner of roast sweet potato and *pitpit*, an asparagus-like plant, and then set up our sleeping gear in an empty hut. I knew I had a hard day ahead of me, but I could not get used to the wooden-plank floor and, worst of all, the constant bombardment of mosquitoes. Covering my head with a jacket didn't help; neither did the aged, torn mosquito net that I wrapped around myself. Frustration and anxiety kept me wide awake, and as the night temperature began to drop, I shuddered and hoped for the morning daylight to come quickly. In the darkness Ken snored peacefully.

Punctually, at daybreak, I thanked Ken for his immense help and set out for Tauna village with eighteen of the twenty Fore cargo carriers — and one scrawny dog — who showed up. I admired the hidden strength of these people, some of whom were only young boys, who toted these forty to fifty pound loads without complaint. None of them looked very strong. They were all rather short and wiry, but their arms and legs just looked like bundles of muscle. They quickly set off in pairs through the *kunai* grassland, and my somewhat faint hope was only to be able to keep up with them. I felt sorry and guilty in the first place for burdening them with my cargo. It made me uncomfortable to think that this might have been a scene out of a typical Hollywood jungle movie where the bwana, in newly-pressed khaki and with pith helmet balanced firmly on his head, leads his "boys" on a safari. I promised myself that I would not give these people the idea that I was a wealthy, authority-struck outsider. But after several decades of direct colonial rule, the Fore attitudes toward the foreigners who ventured into their land, usually demanding work and acquiescence, had already been fixed. Like it or not, I was part of this outside system.

Although I had not slept at all, I stumbled along on sheer excitement. The walk through the grasslands to the rain forest was swift and easy, and to my satisfaction I did not fall once. Then we began to descend. The air lay dank and humid as we approached a low elevation malaria pocket at 2,500 feet. The mosquitoes and other insects increased in density, and all my efforts to brush them away were useless. I never saw what could be identified as a recognizable walking path, so I entrusted myself to the cargo leader, the man with the dog. After passing through the rain forest and then the sharp waist-high grass, we reached one of the small outlets of the Lamari River. Since the water level was low, we crossed it easily, and there the men rested and took short swims to cool off. Along with my cargo, most of them carried their own supplies: bamboo combs, mirrors, and tobacco that they packed into airline travel bags or small *bilums*, woven string bags. Some of these pathetic souvenirs were all the men had to show for their hard years spent as menial indentured laborers on European-owned rubber and copra plantations on the Papua New Guinea coast.

Following the break at the river came the most grueling walk I have ever encountered, far worse than any practice run. Most of the trail was uphill, at what seemed to be a ninety-degree angle. Where the ground was dry, it crumbled under my rubber jungle boots. Where it was wet, I slipped and slid like a broken marionette. When we finally would mount the top of one ridge, another one would be visible in the distance. And then another. The altitude and lack of oxygen in my lungs made the trek virtually unbearable; and I had to stop and rest every hundred feet or so, then fifty feet, then ten feet. I tried to make it easier by thinking that I was just climbing up to the Griffith Observatory in Los Angeles. Unfortunately, most of my body didn't understand.

"How far is Tauna?" I gasped repeatedly. My mouth was as dry as cotton, and my legs felt like rubber crutches. "Close, close," the cargo leader would answer. The small camera around my neck felt like a huge lead weight.

About an hour before actually reaching the village, the cargo carriers began shouting in Fore in the direction of Tauna to announce my presence. Their cries resounded over the mountains, broken only by the shrill cawing of birds. I thought I heard the return calls, or maybe it was just the echoes, but I knew that our final destination must be close.

From the last major hill, the overall view of Tauna did not impress me. I saw no one large grouping of huts. The village was divided into seven small, fence-enclosed hamlets. The furthest ones lay as much as an hour's walk away from each other. The total land area covered about ten square miles, but I could not calculate this accurately because none of the land was level. Most hamlets consisted of from three to ten tiny, circular bamboo-and-grass huts. I saw no one, not even a curious pig, in the first hamlet we passed through. I was puzzled because I had always thought that people would be pleased to have an anthropologist live with them.

Our goal was to reach the *haus kiap*, the small hut in every village where patrol officers and medical assistants stayed during their annual census. In what seemed to be another eternal walk through fast-flowing streams and twisted underbrush when we were actually in Tauna village territory, we finally reached the hut. I no longer felt disappointed. The entire village had assembled there to greet me and inspect my cargo.

The nearly two hundred men, women, and children approached me from every direction, shouting, laughing, and noisily pelting me with questions in Awa. Most of the children and women wore only their traditional bark skirts. The men were dressed in either ragged store-bought shorts or dirty *laplaps*. Most had no shirts. None wore shoes. Through this all I could smell the stench of dirt, sweat, and rancid pig grease on some of their bodies. But all I could concentrate on for the

TAUNA VILLAGE AND HAMLETS

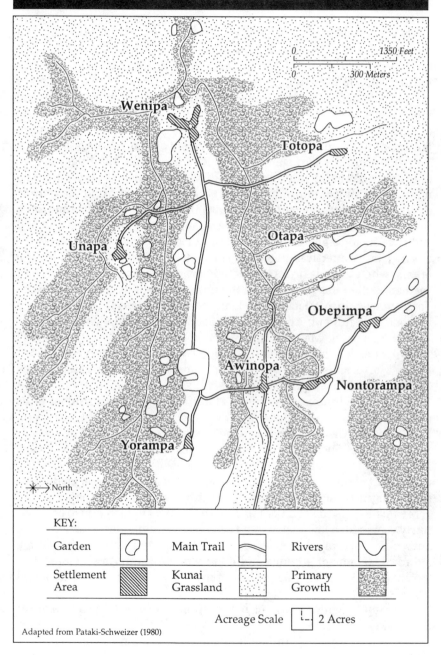

Wenipa

Totopa

Unapa

Otapa

Obepimpa

Awinopa

Nontorampa

Yorampa

✳⟶North

0   1350 Feet

0   300 Meters

KEY:

| Garden | Main Trail | Rivers |
| Settlement Area | Kunai Grassland | Primary Growth |

Acreage Scale   2 Acres

Adapted from Pataki-Schweizer (1980)

moment were the painful blisters on my feet and the dozens of red slashes that had appeared on my legs from brushing against the sharp *kunai* grass.

My knees buckled beneath me, and I knelt down completely exhausted on the dirt floor. A single stream of light peeked through the opening of the shabby, darkened hut. My bare legs ached and creaked from the torturous mountain walk, and I could not even savor the luxury of a few seconds of silence to collect my thoughts. Slowly the buzz of flies and mosquitoes built up, collaborating with the fleas that danced peskily around my ankles. With the crowd outside, chattering and pointing, I felt completely out of place, like a prize specimen in a zoo.

"*Klia! Klia!*" I heard someone shout in Tok Pisin, the lingua franca of the area. From the middle of the noisy, gawking spectators, a man no more than five feet tall in his bare feet pushed his way into the narrow opening of the hut. He parted the crowd in the manner of someone quite important. He wore a black *laplap*, a wraparound cloth sarong cinched at the waist, and a green sweatshirt. I saw that his clothes were impeccably clean. His manner was guarded, somewhat different from that of the others, who ran their fingers enviously over my suitcases and boxes and seemed to me pushy. He offered me a pleasant smile, which had worn deep grooves in his face around his nose and mouth. Handing me a bamboo tube full of fresh drinking water, he addressed me in Tok Pisin: "Good afternoon, Master. Can I wash your clothes?"

That question shocked and offended me. Immediately he placed himself in a subservient, obsequious position by addressing me as "Master" and by volunteering his services.

I had traveled thousands of miles to this village to be a student of its culture, not some obnoxious outsider who demanded to be waited on hand and foot. Clean clothes were the last thing on my mind. I welcomed, however, the chance to try out my rudimentary Pisin on a friendly face, hoping that I would be able to communicate with someone, anyone. The man squatted down on his haunches and prepared a cigarette made from store-bought twist tobacco and a discarded scrap of newspaper.

My Pisin-speaking companion's name was Ila. I judged him to be about thirty years old, a few years older than me. He summoned a dozen young boys, some only eight or nine years old, to line up in front of me for my approval as potential household helpers. Not wanting to be taken advantage of in the very beginning of my stay, I tried to appear calm and collected.

"I'll wait a while. I haven't made up my mind yet," I mumbled in broken Pisin.

Ila saw my insecurity, and without any suggestion he bolted to his feet and chased the curious children outside. He returned to his cigarette.

In the clearing outside the door a fierce, balding warrior about sixty years old pointed to my cargo boxes and began shouting in Awa, the local language that I could not understand. He wore only a torn pair of shorts. His copper-colored skin, covered with a film of dirt and sweat, glistened in the late afternoon sun.

"That's Api," Ila said. "He is my *kandere*, a relative on my mother's side. He is the number one Big Man (traditional political leader) of the village."

"What is he saying?" I asked impatiently.

"He says that he has plenty goods, many pigs, and sweet potato gardens. He has a wife and six children. He says that you have nothing."

I wondered seriously if I would ever get to know this stern warrior. I came to know later that he was a man who had fought many bloody battles against other villages; he had fired on the first white men who passed through the village twenty years before. I knew from previous studies of Papua New Guinea that as a village Big Man he had gained his high position by his personal charisma and power, his oratory, connections with other men, strategic skills, and his ability to win the respect people showed him. In short, he was an accomplished leader.

Only one generation separated Ila and Api, but while Ila had had firsthand experience in the white man's world, Api had not. I could see these differences quite clearly in their knowledge of Pisin and in their age, clothes, and mannerisms.

Ila continued to comfort me with his presence and small talk. Outside, Api kept up his harangue in Awa, occasionally casting me an icy glare.

Chapter 2

Dancing in the Dark

I could see that Ila was well liked and respected by the other villagers. Intuitively, I felt that he understood me and my purpose more than anyone else. With those characteristics, I was sure that he would make an excellent key informant, a person on whom I could rely. But I didn't want to appear to be too eager in my choice.

After hesitating deliberately, I turned to him and said, "You speak Tok Pisin well. Mine is bad, and I know nothing yet about Awa. Maybe you can translate for me and tell me stories about your ancestors."

He nodded at my suggestion with the air of great confidence, as if it were routine work that he had done many times before. "I know this kind of work," he said confidently. "I know what you want. I have worked for masters in Port Moresby, Rabaul, Kavieng, Buka, and Kainantu. I like the fashion of the white man. They have plenty of clothes, money, and big houses. They eat good food. No one else knows the work of masters like I do. I am the only man in this village who can do this." I was convinced that Ila was earnest and sincere.

By evening most of the people, satiated with the novelty of my presence, walked up or down the steep slopes to their huts for their meals of sweet potato and vegetable greens. Those who remained continued to ask me the same questions I had answered over and over: Are you a missionary? How long will you stay? Where will you live? What is your name? Where is your wife? Will you open a store? Why don't you hire me to work for you?

Ila, already my unofficial go-between, sat closest to me in the hut. He was the last to say good night and promised me he would begin work early in the morning.

My head spun from the excitement, or perhaps it was simply the altitude. Hunger and fatigue began to set in. I worried about Jackie walking in the next day because of the severe climb. I sat alone in the darkness of the hut, which was illuminated only by some stubborn embers, when an old woman stopped by from her garden to offer me a bunch of raw peanuts pulled directly from the ground. She muttered something to me in Awa that I could not understand. This was my first meal and my first night in the village. It certainly had to get better than this. Finally, in the dark silence, I fell asleep uncovered on the dirt floor.

Early the next morning, not much after the roosters began their crowing, Ila walked right into the hut, surprising me. He was in a good mood and inhaled casually on his usual newspaper-and-tobacco cigarette. I stood up to greet him on my sore, shaky legs.

"Good morning," I said.

"*Gu moni,*" he echoed in Pisin. "Can I wash your clothes?"

There must be something to his insistence, I thought, so I gave in. I folded up a bundle of dirty clothes and handed him a brush and full bar of soap. Perhaps this would help our newly defined relationship. I was a little disturbed that he had volunteered so quickly to do menial work. I wanted us to be closer, more on equal terms if possible. But that could not be as long as I was the master and he was the *boi*. Based on his experiences as a former laborer in the coastal towns of Papua New Guinea, Ila's response was quite predictable. There, deference was demanded.

I sat and waited as the people, now including some from more distant villages, again began to crowd inside the dingy hut to throw me some new questions and repeat the old ones.

Several hours later Ila returned with the old clothes, which he had hung dry and neatly folded, and the brush.

"Where's the bar of soap?" I asked.

"It slipped out of my hand and floated down the river," he replied, somewhat taken aback that I had even noticed. For my benefit he even went through the gestures of scrubbing and chasing the soap.

I did not want to make this a major issue. I knew I was being tested as to how easy I would be with my possessions, but I also knew that I could not afford to relinquish a bar of soap every time a few things needed washing. I had to draw the line quickly, just to survive in the village with my goods intact. Already some of the men had claimed most of my possessions—including my typewriter and camera—for themselves when I would eventually leave the village. Ila himself chose most of my clothes, especially a red T-shirt that he would often come in to glare at and touch.

I turned to Ila and said, "Next time, hang on to the soap more carefully, or else someone else will have to do the job." It was a tone of voice that I was not accustomed to using. Ila half-smiled, as a defense for his embarrassment, and glanced down at the ground. My obvious irritation and his response made us both feel uneasy.

For my own balance, I did not want to depend solely on Ila for information or for work. As I was becoming aware of this, Kawo, a young married man about Ila's age and one of the only other village men who was fluent in Pisin, walked into the hut for a chat.

Kawo and Ila were cousins. Of the two, Kawo was stockier, more muscular, and lighter-skinned than Ila. Kawo's wide smile revealed a set of red-stained teeth, which Ila did not have, from years of chewing betel, a mixture of the areca nut, leaves, and lime that has discolored many mouths from Melanesia to Nepal.

"Gu moni, Tewe [David]," he greeted me informally. Although the villagers had learned my name, none except Kawo so far called me that. To the rest I was still Master, or Mata, as they pronounced it. Kawo was different. He didn't show an intense curiosity about my cargo, nor did he deign to beg for menial work.

"I would like a cigarette," he said forcefully. I placed one in his hand, along with a box of matches, which he stuck in his shirt pocket. Unlike Ila and most of the others, Kawo didn't greet me with much enthusiasm. He simply seemed resigned to my presence in Tauna and would make the best of it. Addressing me by my first name ironically, was not intended to get close to me; it was more to keep a respectful, equal distance between us. Like Ila, Kawo had worked on the copra and rubber plantations of the coast and had seen his share of the master-boi relationship.

"You will need a house for you and your wife when she arrives," Kawo said. "You can pay me to organize the work crew. There is a good spot down below. Come outside; you can see it from there." About 300 yards down a winding footpath in a cleared hamlet, I could see Ila's small rectangular house, a miniature copy of a European dwelling, and four or five of the traditional, windowless round huts of Tauna.

"Let's take a closer look," I said eagerly. Kawo leading the way, we walked down to the hamlet. We first chose one site but discovered the ground was not level enough.

"There. Over there," Kawo pointed. "We can tear down that old hut and build your house there. The ground is straight."

"Fine," I said. "I would like you to build me a large, rectangular house and a separate cooking house." To make my point, which I couldn't quite convey in my limited Pisin, I picked up a stick and drew a diagram on the ground.

Kawo reassured me. "I know . . . a white man's kind of house." The he lapsed into a loud lecture in Awa, directed to everyone standing around. Its meaning, I guessed, was to form a work group to gather building materials, namely bamboo, *pitpit* stalks, and *kunai* grass. Every so often I heard the Pisin word for *money.*

Kawo and I agreed that the location of the house would be at the downhill end of a small hamlet called Nontorampa. Along with Kawo, Ila lived there, as did four other families. It was a good spot on relatively level ground, and an icy-cold stream for bathing and drinking water was only a hundred feet away. The land itself belonged to Kawo's clan, and it was agreed that he would inherit the house when we left.

Throughout the day, many of the men from Tauna and even other villages sought me out. Although the older men were curious about me, they usually just strolled by nonchalantly in their cloth G-strings or old, tattered shorts. A few came to shake hands and hiss "Shhhh, shhhh" as a sign of friendly acknowledgement. I noticed that Api, who probably deeply resented my presence, avoided me completely. The Awa women, none of whom spoke Pisin, were also reserved. The children were friendly and exuberant, but always cautious. Kawo liked to play on their fear by grabbing a young boy, speaking sternly to him in Awa, and then pointing at me as if I were some kind of menacing monster. Invariably, the child would burst into tears and scramble back to his mother in absolute terror. Kawo and the other men found these jokes hilarious.

Only the young men, especially those who had worked away from the Highlands, on the coast, knew the ways of the outsiders firsthand. They used a variety of approaches. Some stood around for fifteen minutes before blurting out a request. Others sidled up to me, looking about furtively, as if to present me with a bargain I could not refuse. They all wanted the same thing: to be put on the work crew for the house. But I left that decision up to Kawo, who unashamedly first appointed all his fellow clan-mates, then his wife's clansmen, and finally his friends.

"They will work hard. They are not rubbish men," Kawo assured me.

The Awa neither read nor write, but Kawo insisted that I write down their names on a sheet of paper. This was to "officially" certify their promise to work on the house. It was something the government officers always did. Left without work, some of the other men wanted to teach me to grow sweet potatoes, hunt wild pigs with bows and arrows, and speak Awa. They all believed that I was a ready source of money. The problem, however, was that I was deluged with too many zealous volunteers. Friends brought in friends, relatives brought in relatives. Many of the people were from distant outside villages. But I made no concrete plans with any of them. Knowing nothing yet about their all-important kinship relationships, I did not want to favor some people and leave others out.

After several hours of discussion over the formation of the work group, I became weary by the constant barrage of pleading. To make matters worse, it began to rain; and within several minutes a slight drizzle turned into a monsoon-like downpour. Soon it would be pitch black, that complete darkness that envelopes the rain forest, and Jackie had not yet arrived. I had kept my eye on the footpaths that led high into the surrounding mountains, but I saw and heard nothing all day.

Then some muffled cries.

"Tauna-o. Tauna-o. Tauna-ooo." Ila called me outside. He pointed with his chin to the distant hills to the west. That was a completely different direction than the one I had come in from the day before. "Look! Look! The missus is there."

I saw what appeared to be about a dozen figures on a distant hill. They looked like small ants crawling down a vine. I could hear the announcement calls of the fore carriers getting louder and the shouts of Awa answering them. Gradually, through the growing mountain mist and rain, details became sharper. I recognized some of the Fore cargo carriers as the same men who had come with me the day before!

Jackie's party had trudged into the village through the well-known shortcut. Almost all of it ran either straight uphill or downhill. From Okasa, where Ken and I camped, a small footpath leads to a wide tributary of the Lamari River. There the road winds several thousand feet upward into the adjacent Auyana-speaking village of Kawaina, and then the narrow footpath zigzags straight downward through dense untouched rain forest into Tauna.

At about two hundred yards, when I could clearly see Jackie and the carriers, Ila grabbed my umbrella and raced up the hill for her. This was a touching symbolic gesture, but functionally useless. She, as well as the carriers, were soaked to the core and caked with mud up to their knees. On the final leg of the trip, Yagai, a handsome, muscular policeman from the Okapa station, carried Jackie in on his back.

I felt such a great sense of relief within me. Jackie and I looked for some privacy, just for a moment, to hold each other. But again the pointing and questioning began and continued unbroken until nightfall. Finally, alone in the shadows of the hut, we laughed out loud in a long embrace. But there was little time. We set up our mosquito nets and stuffed two canvas sleeping sleeves with kunai grass to make them more comfortable. I paid the Fore carriers and off they went again, seemingly indestructible, tireless men, disappearing into the night air.

Yagai, looking completely unfazed in his blue shorts and shirt, beret, and black ankle boots, stayed behind. The only thing I could offer him was a tin of cold beef stew for dinner. He chose not to eat with us, I think somehow feeling that his place was with Ila, Kawo, and their friends in

Nontorampa hamlet. We ravaged a tin of cold corned beef and gnawed on a stick of raw sugar cane. That was all we had to eat ourselves.

More than anything we needed a permanent house to live, but unending delays in building it seemed to arise. Usually, the heavy afternoon rains from the west stopped the work completely, and the village leaders, in their interpretation of the edicts of the Australian administration, discouraged any active labor on Sundays, which was defined as the day of rest.

For house-building supplies, I had bought twenty pounds of nails and several hammers and a saw. But most of the time the men used their own implements and ingenuity, carving out the frame posts with old, dull two-foot-long machetes. Many of the nails simply vanished. I discovered later that the men wore them out, sticking them in their hair like porcupine needles; and I suspected that they would later be used to strengthen their own huts.

I made it a point to personally supervise the developing outline of the house. It was to be rectangular rather than round, for more space. Down the middle would be a small hallway, to the right a partitioned sleeping room, and on the left my work room. Its base measured about twelve by twenty feet. In Goroka, I also purchased a roll of clear plastic so that windows could be fitted into various walls to draw in the daily sunlight. Having heard horror stories of anthropologists losing their valuable field notes in fires, I also contracted the builders to build a separate cook house, off to the side of the main structure.

Some of the women wanted to work and earn money, and their job, supervised by the watchful eyes of Kawo, was to chop, collect, and bundle the kunai and pitpit, the reedy grasses that were lashed together to form the roof and sidewalls.

Several days passed, and the house slowly began to take shape. The stumpy foundation posts set the woven bamboo floor about two feet above the ground. Long, vertical posts towered ten feet high, double the height of the conical roofs of their own round huts. One uncharacteristic sunny afternoon I walked down to the hamlet to check on the house's progress. I thought I stepped deftly over the fence, which was built high enough to keep the domestic pigs out of the compound, and headed toward Kawo, who was crushing a dark green, twenty-foot length of bamboo. I didn't know that the recent rain had turned the cleared hamlet floor into a slick skating rink.

"Kawo. How is the . . .?" I couldn't finish my question. My right foot slid to the side, and then I tumbled uncontrollably down a small, slippery mound into a pool of fresh mud. The entire work crew and everyone else turned and stared.

Rarely seeing anyone make such a clumsy move, something no three-year-old in the local culture would do, the work crew did not know what reaction to show—sympathy, worry, or plain pity. Sheepishly, I looked around for some hidden obstacle to blame. I didn't know how to act either. A muddy brown stripe caked my entire right side from head to toe. Ila rushed toward me sympathetically, suppressing the urge to burst out laughing. Kawo, keeping more distant than Ila, stayed in place; and when I propped myself up, I could see his glistening red teeth flashing an almost pleasurable smile. That accident, more than any other good intention or smile, had broken the ice. I felt that most of them now saw me in a more human light. I too was just a man—an outsider, but not one who was protected with the untouchable cloak of authority. I was vulnerable.

The house was vulnerable also, to slowdowns. Among other things, selling coffee beans delayed work on it. When men from Tauna returned from short labor stints outside the village in the early 1960s, some of them brought coffee plants back with them. Ila and Kawo were among the first group of Awa villagers to leave voluntarily, to pick the red, ripe coffee berries on European-owned coffee plantations in Kainantu. After picking and pulping coffee berries for several months, they returned to Tauna with their new experiences and told the others of the enormity of the white man's cargo and the power of his money. Ila and Kawo learned Tok Pisin quickly enough to talk to these strange, pale outsiders whom their elders, only a few short years ago, believed to be the ghosts of returned ancestors.

Coffee and money, money and coffee became the new twins of success. Soon the traditional forms of Awa wealth, cowrie shells and rare bird feathers, lost their importance. Within the culture that created it, the old wealth became museum pieces. Money and store-bought goods increasingly became the most important tokens of exchange in all right-of-passage transactions, including birth, male initiation, marriage, and death.

Persistently lured, perhaps seduced, by outside work, money, coffee, and stores, the men and women would no longer live their lives as self-sufficient subsistence horticulturalists. These long-independent villagers, whether they liked it or not and whether they knew it or not, fell to the bottom of a new social hierarchy. Government politicians and some anthropologists called them *rural minorities* or *incipient peasants*. *Development* and *Melanesian unity* were the new watchwords, and they tolled along with the ringing clarion call of eventual political independence.

In reality, however, many distant, roadless, Fourth World people like the Awa saw their visions turn sour. To many, they were just another backward people to look down on and shame because of their traditional ways. Most of the colonial bureaucrats saw it this way, as did every other tribal group who thought themselves to be somewhat advanced according to the outside world's scales of progress.

Ila, especially, and Kawo took to growing coffee instantly. With their money they bought clothing, tins of fish and meat bags of rice, and household tools as soon as they could. The new materialism appealed both to their minds and bellies.

And from this, many tribesmen, particularly those around government stations, were able to bypass centuries of Western technological development. They tuned in their Japanese-made transistor radios, bounced around in the latest Toyota pickup trucks, and wore jogging shoes and stylish athletic outfits. One could see this surrealistic collage of imported goods overlaying traditional culture on many backroads throughout the Highlands.

Not everyone in Tauna showed enthusiasm about growing coffee. Many elderly Big Men, like Api, flatly rejected the idea. Why would they want to cultivate an imported crop that they could not eat? If they needed money, they could always borrow or extract it from the younger men through bridewealth demands or exchange debts. It was not so much the inoffensive little berries themselves as the fact that they symbolized the encroaching, powerful, and unknown outside world.

Every few months, half of the villagers packed up their husked, dried, and cleaned coffee berries, stuffed them into their expandable string bags, and carted them on their heads to the end of the vehicular road near the wet pine forest. There a buyer like Ken would weigh and pay them for each bag. Sometimes the buyer would sell them back matches, cigarettes, bags of rice, oily, red perfume, tins of mackerel or corned beef, or clothing for their hard-earned money.

Villagers were supposed to be paid about ten cents (U.S.) for a pound of dried coffee beans. But unscrupulous local or European buyers would often pay them far less, knowing that they could not read the weight scale or multiply coffee pounds by cents. Exploited all around, the villagers had no bargaining rights, and it would have been senseless for them to lug their coffee beans back to the village in protest. They did, however, gossip among themselves about the differences between good and bad buyers. For all the labor of planting coffee, shelling the berries, and toting fifty-pound sacks to the road on their heads, their earnings were minuscule. Some relatively wealthy men like Ila, who grew many coffee trees, demonstrated a keen sense of business by paying younger boys and girls to carry his coffee sacks to the road.

Most of the village men owned at least one pair of store-bought shorts and wore them until they were dirty, frazzled strips of torn cloth. Some sported new T-shirts and colorful cotton shirts. But most of the women had no regular source of income. Some had planted coffee, but none had worked outside the village. Only women whose husbands sold coffee and were generous could afford to buy the trade stores' gimcrack trinkets.

These they wore on festive occasions and when the annual census patrol arrived.

Because so many people of the village were gone on a coffee-selling expedition, the house building stopped completely. The small children, naked or wearing only short bark pubic coverings, played running games in the hamlet until the oppressive heat of the afternoon. The elderly and infirm napped in the cool darkness of their huts. Those who remained worked in their gardens and were made invisible by the dense rain forest canopy. Ila sent his younger hirelings to do the heavy coffee work and stayed behind.

"I would like to learn to understand Awa," I announced to Ila in the silent, private afternoon.

He shrugged approvingly. "Yes. It is my work to teach. I am ready to begin."

Awa is a complex tonal language genetically related to Auyana, Gadsup, and Tairora, tongues spoken by the peoples to the north and east. I got some help from a short dictionary by Dick Loving, a missionary-linguist. He had lived intermittently with the Awa of Mobutah village for about a dozen years.

I sat down cross-legged on the ground inside our hut and thumbed through the dictionary.

"*Topah*," I said slowly, trying to remember the most general term for sweet potato.

"*Topah*," Ila repeated quickly.

"*Porah*." This means pig, I thought to myself.

"Yes. You are learning the most important words," Ila added with a grin.

Fortunately for my language study, Ila was not only familiar with the other three dialects of Awa spoken in the southern villages, but he also knew Auyana, the language of the Kawaina people directly up the hill from Tauna. He obviously preferred this kind of thought work to working on the house. "I am like you," he said. "My work is with talk."

But for both of us the elementary language work was slow and laborious. After a half hour Ila began to fidget, staring out the opening of the hut and chain-smoking. I put down the dictionary and changed the subject.

"I'd like to talk together every day, at least once a day. Sometimes we will talk from the dictionary, and other times we will just discuss what happened in the village." My Pisin at least was improving rapidly.

"Yes, yes," Ila agreed.

"What I want to start soon is to find out about all of your relatives and ancestors and all those of everyone in Tauna. I especially want to know about the elderly Big Men and who their ancestors were, what fights they had with other villages in the past, and . . . "

Ila broke in. "Yes. I know all of that." He grew more interested. "And I will bring down Api; he lives at Yorampa, that hamlet on the hill above us."

Ila paused and grinned. "He talked to the people about you when you first sat down here with all your cargo." He laughed again at that incident. "Whatever I don't know, Api does. You will meet him later."

Work on the house continued to proceed slowly. It seemed that daily verbal fights between Kawo, the women, and the workers from other villages always seemed to flare up.

"You men hurry up and set up the posts before it rains!" Kawo bellowed. "You women get some more *kunai* grass for the roof! This is not work for nothing. This is work for money!"

To say that each man made up his own mind would be a gross understatement. Ignoring Kawo's exhortations, some of the men sat by idly, smoking and talking and complaining of pains. Others disappeared into the bush, only to return with a small bundle of bamboo for an entire day's outing. The house-building factions also fomented the decades of previous antagonism that had built up between the Tauna men and the workers from Tawaina, the closest Awa village to the east. The old history of suspicion and mutual, hostile chicanery short-circuited many tempers.

The Tauna men wanted to be the only ones to work on the house for the simple reason that they sought to keep the money they would earn in their own village. But as a favor to the government councillor from Tawaina, Kawo hired some of those men to help.

The old councillor usually just sat around, watching the house take shape and puffing on a bamboo pipe stuffed with acrid, home-grown tobacco. There was no doubt that he was still a crafty warrior. As a councillor—a modern political leader elected by his own people—he was nominally in charge of keeping peace in the three clustered Awa villages of Tauna, Tawaina, and Ilakia. If major trouble of any kind occurred, he was to report it immediately to Peter Broadhurst in Okapa or to any other patrol officer at the station, as they called Okapa. Abate, the councillor, could usually be seen sitting in the shade of a banana tree, his green, battered Australian bush hat tipped slightly to the side, displaying a metal badge stamped Councillor Territory of Papua New Guinea. He made sure that Kawo did not mishandle or fire any of the men from his village.

Despite these squabbles, everyone wanted to finish the house in time for the annual census patrol from Okapa, due to arrive in less than a week. The men desperately needed to collect their wages from me in order to pay the recently imposed government head tax. This money was to be used for roads, schools, and other development projects in the Okapa District. Coffee or no coffee, work or no work, every adult man n the village had to pay the tax. In Tauna it stood at $6 a man.

Our rat-infested, insect-ridden temporary hut never really felt like home. One clear, dry night, the faint drone of distant chanting aroused me from my uncomfortable half-sleep. It came from the direction of Obepimpa hamlet, home of the Obepina clan, ten minutes' walk up a narrow dirt footpath. I stepped outside into the darkness and turned my head to listen. Like an errie, nocturnal choir, it started again and then stopped. This went on for several hours. Because it would have been extremely difficult for me to walk to Obepimpa in the blackness, I went back to bed and decided to wait until morning to find out what it was all about.

When Ila walked into the hut in the morning, I immediately pounced on him. "What was that singing last night? You must always tell be beforehand when anything like this is going to happen. That's why I'm here, you know."

Answering indirectly, he asked, "Do you want to hear some more?"

"Yes, yes. Of course," I replied enthusiastically.

"Then the dancers will do it again this evening, before dark. This time they will do it right here in front of your hut. They will dance until they are tired. I will send them up myself to make sure they come."

I was immensely excited. This would be my first close-up look at an authentic traditional ritual. Until now, life with the Awa had been difficult but rather mundane. The house building and bickering had nothing to do with anthropology, as far as I was concerned.

8:00 P.M. No one showed up. I waited.

9:00 P.M. Except for a few grunting pigs thrashing through the bush, the night air was silent. Even Ila was nowhere to be seen.

11:30 P.M. Still more irritating silence. I was upset. Did he deliberately lie to me? Was I being tested, as some anthropologists had told me I would be?

When nothing stirred by midnight, I gave up waiting. Sometime later, perhaps it was an hour, our sleep was broken abruptly by a dozen young boys and girls who, in quick bursts of singing and dancing, came to reenact their dance in front of the hut.

Groggy and testy, I found my enthusiasm had waned. But even in my disappointment that they had not appeared when Ila said they would (a lesson about time that I was to learn over and over), I slid out of the canvas sleeping sleeve and sat down outside. I saw a dozen figures pacing up and down in the dim moonlight. Most of the boys wore their usual torn shorts and shirts. The girls had bark cloth skirts. Foot-long, green *tanket* leaves covered their buttocks. I vaguely made out what they were doing. They marched thirty feet up, then back, repeating this movement over and over. All the while they chanted what seemed to be multiple versions of the same song.

I could neither see very clearly nor understand what was going on, but I remembered a strategy suggested to me by an anthropologist who learned that I had planned to do fieldwork in Papua New Guinea. He said that I should watch a game or any other kind of patterned behavior that I was unfamiliar with, like cricket, and attempt to discover the *rules* by watching what the people did. Before me was a similar puzzle. Still it had no meaning to me. What were they doing? And why? What were the rules?

I reminded myself to question Ila in the morning about the precise significance and symbolism of the dance.

The dance ended after an hour, when everyone seemed to be exhausted. They had kept Ila's promise. But I could not sleep. Morning did not come soon enough. I was anxious to talk to Ila, and I walked down to his hut, stepping lively with my unfulfilled curiosity. I wanted to know everything about the meanings of the songs and the ritual intricacies I had witnessed.

"Why did they pace back and forth so many times? What was the reason for the dance?" I held back my desire to ask more questions and, taking my clean notebook and pen in hand, I waited to collect my first real piece of ethnographic field data.

Ila casually puffed out a whiff of smoke from his cigarette and shrugged his shoulders. "It was nothing," he said flatly. "They did it for nothing." He then excused himself and headed toward his taro garden.

Collecting data by using a single key informant is a hit-and-miss affair. Adjustments have to be made on both sides. Often Ila's thoughts seemed to me to drift elsewhere. When he tired of my questions, he tried to change the subject to things he liked to talk about. When bored, he stared out blankly into space and curtly answered my questions with just a yes or no. Sometimes he impatiently shook his legs back and forth, knocking his knees, as if he were sitting on top of a campfire. His attention span for my academic interests lasted about an hour at most, usually only fifteen minutes. To prolong his interest I offered him cigarette after cigarette which he requested; I flattered him; and I hinted that he would be the eventual recipient of many of our household goods. This, I knew, was sheer bribery, but I didn't know what else to do.

When he decided the interviewing time was up, he would often offer me cues, dismissing me with "I'm tired now" or "I've got to look over my new coffee garden on that hill."

I discovered that Ila had a highly manipulable image. One face for me, one face for them. Although he always told me he was hurrying the women to collect the *kunai* grass for the roof, he always yelled at them with a grin on his face that neutralized his verbal threats. He took the side of anyone who was cross with him. Ila was a born politician. But I also knew that when these distant villagers met and spoke with outsiders, including anthropologists, they never displayed the upper hand, having already been controlled in more ways than one by a generation of colonial contact.

Ila sat insecurely between an old way of life, which he saw to be doomed, and a new one that captured his interest but would never fully be his own. There were just too many barriers, some of which he barely knew about, standing in the way: formal eduction, language, wealth, geography, ethnicity.

It was when I understood this — and I don't think I was simply projecting — that I felt that Ila and I were very much alike. We both seemed to take an odd, detached view of our own respective cultures, standing somewhat askew, not being entirely in step with everyone else. I saw much of myself in Ila.

But in many ways he was far more accomplished than I: his observational and descriptive skills, his memory, his facility for languages, his story-telling ability, his tactful relationships with almost everyone. He was a natural anthropologist; I was trying to be taught. Only the perverse fortunes of birth and opportunity brought me to study his culture.

Chapter 3

Between Two Worlds

When six days had passed, a sturdy young Australian *kiap* bounded down the narrow footpath that leads from the Auyana-language village of Kawaina. A team of a dozen cargo carriers trailed behind him. Patrol officers do not travel lightly. Census records, chairs, tables, kerosene lamps, teapots, food, clothes, and a carefully folded Australian flag all had to be packed, unpacked, and stuffed back into metal cargo boxes. Sean had come from the Okapa station to visit each of the Auyana, South Fore, and Awa villages. His purpose was to record the census, collect the mandatory head tax, and adjudicate any current court cases, the most prominent of which in Tauna was a heated adultery dispute.

Anto, an outraged, cuckolded husband, had been keeping a running tally of his young wife's infidelities by tying knots on a length of twine which he carried in his string bag. The third party was Konato, a married man who had spent several years on coastal plantations and had adopted many recent fashions of the urban scene. He usually wore a pair of clean dark shorts and a colorful cotton short-sleeved shirt. A pair of sunglasses perched on top of his head. Konato looked more like a tourist coming in from the sun than an Awa sweet potato farmer.

Konato and young, demure Taiya had consensually engaged in sexual intercourse a total of thirteen times as proven by Anto's knots. In the course of hearing the facts of the case, Sean had discovered that Konato had been

37

An outdoor court with Kawo (second from right) presiding.

paying "tax" money to Kawo and Abate, the old councillor. Only two days earlier they collected $5 from him. Taking advantage of their official positions as councillor and committeeman, Abate and Kawo had been illegally fining many of the villagers, including their own relatives. Whenever they heard that someone had committed an offense, whether it be pig stealing or wife beating, they levied a fine on the offender and put the money in their own pockets. If the offender did not pay, they threatened him with jail or severe physical punishment at the hands of the Australian patrol officers.

When Sean heard of this extortion and bold misuse of authority, he promptly wrote out a citation for both the old councillor and Kawo. They were to return the $5 to Konato and appear before a judge in Okapa within a week. The adultery complaint found no quick, satisfactory outcome and would have to wait.

The following morning, Sean left with a dozen Tauna men for Tawaina, the next Awa village to the east. The village assumed a strange silence. Ila tried to excuse himself because of his work with me, but that didn't impress the *kiap*. He simply saw another able-bodied carrier. Although a few of the traditional Big Men were elderly, they, too, acquiesced without resistance and staggered under the weight of the metal cargo boxes. I saw them trudge single file up the Tawaiwa road. The thought of perhaps being an indirect accomplice to these once-independent villagers now turning into slavish cargo boys brought on in me a feeling of horrendous guilt.

Kawo was the only person who was exempt. He confided in me that that sort of menial labor was humiliating and would have been an affront to his status in the village.

"I am a committeeman," he said. "I am not just a man who takes care of his pigs and gardens. Carrying cargo is fine for the young boys and men who have no money and no thoughts. But I am different."

That was the first time I became aware of the deeply buried feelings Kawo had for the way the village men, and sometimes the women, were indiscriminately rounded up, often abused, and paid a pittance for a hard day's work. Kawo was clearly (if silently) outraged with being pushed around, especially in his own domain. The official government authority was something he had to live with, but he did not have to accept everything about it.

Kawo and I stood in the spot where an hour before the Australian flag had fluttered in the wind at the top of a bamboo flag pole. He rolled a cigarette from the dried home-grown tobacco leaves he kept folded in his shirt pocket and a scrap of newspaper I handed him. There was a long pause: I knew he had something else he wanted to talk about.

"Tewe," he said quietly. "I want you to write a letter for me." He looked around slowly to see if anyone was in hearing range.

I replied without hesitation. "Of course. Come inside. I'll write it on the machine." "Who's it for?" I asked.

"I want it to go to Master Peter, the number one *kiap* in Okapa. I do not want to go to jail or court. I want him to understand why I taxed people."

"Okay. Go ahead," I encouraged him.

He dictated his words slowly and thoughtfully. "Master Peter," he began. "I taxed people to give money to my sister who doesn't have any. I didn't keep the money for myself. I am going to earn money by building a house for Tewe. That's all. My name is Kawo."

I rolled the note out of the typewriter and handed it to him. "Do you have a skin for it?" he asked. I gave him a clean envelope. He thanked me and abruptly left the hut with the letter tucked carefully in his shirt pocket against the tobacco leaves.

The Awa saw literacy as a mysterious, yet impressive, power. Letters could "talk" to distant places where people could "hear" them and even send back replies. Writing and reading were also seen to be a ritual necessity of the government bureaucracy in Okapa and the ways of the white authorities. So in matters that the villagers considered to be of official importance, I usually acted as their gladly accommodating scribe.

That night the rain poured down uncontrollably. Powerful clashes of thunder barreled over the hills. White spiny fingers of lightning shattered the sky. It was bad enough that the loud patter on the roof and bamboo walls kept us awake, but the strong winds angled the stream of water through the walls onto our sleeping bags. The heavy rain brought on another irritant: the hungry, squeaking, nocturnal rodents that came scampering into the hut and over our dozing bodies in search of food.

When Ila returned from the Tawaina patrol, I told him of our nightly intruders. "I know what to do," he said. He immediately began work on an ancient ingenious contraption made from a two-foot length of bamboo tubing, an arched twig, and some twine. Using small pieces of raw sweet potato as bait, he set three traps around the sides of the hut. I was a little skeptical when I went to sleep that night.

The next morning I walked out of the hut to examine the traps. Rats had still come into the hut at night. Each of the traps had been sprung, and I could see the long tails and hind legs of the rats sticking out from the bamboo tubes! From then on, trap setting became a regular part of our nightly ritual before going to sleep. And each morning the children would come along to see how many rats we had caught. Whatever we caught, I gave away. They ran off cackling, grasping the carcasses firmly around the bellies with their tight little fists. In the dark privacy of their own huts, they scorched them lightly over the fire and consumed them along with their usual breakfast of roast sweet potato.

The traps, however, were not entirely foolproof. Often, a rat would be caught by a looped twine around the waist or leg, and it would squeal and run helplessly in circles while it was attached to the bamboo and twine chain. Awakened by the shrieks of the half-trapped rats, I would have to pull myself out of the sleeping bag each night and swiftly do them in with a sharp machete. There were not too many nights in my entire stay when I did not have to get up at least once to finish off a squealing, wounded rat, dispose of it outside, and reset the traps. It became almost a game to see how many could be killed in one night, and for a short time I even kept score. (The all-time nightly record was seven.) The children, of course, were delighted with our devotion to this task.

One morning at the beginning of an interviewing session, I presented Ila with what I knew would be a sensitive question. "How do you like the taste of roast rat?" I asked, studying his reaction.

"No, no," he protested, slightly shocked. "Grown-up men and women do not eat that. It is *tambu*. Only the children can do this because they don't yet have the thoughts of the elders."

"But what about Tiara, the old lady in that hut?" I pointed out. "I saw her eating some with the children only yesterday."

Grudgingly Ila admitted, "Yes. Some of the older people eat it, but they are 'bush' people. They follow the old ways. They don't know the good taste of tinned meat and fish and rice, things that the white men eat. They are the people from before."

Although Ila was referring to some of his own kinsmen as "bushy," including his clan mates and in-laws, he obviously meant to set himself apart from them. Of course he was an Awa Highlander, but now he was more than that. He had unloaded the huge transport ships lining the harbor in Port Moresby; he had ironed clothes and cooked for an Australian family living in Rabaul; he had drunk beer with lonely plantation mates in Kavieng; he had carried cargo for the *kiap* throughout the Eastern Highlands from Kainantu to Wonenara. Few Awa men had spent as much time away from the Highlands as he, and almost no Awa woman or elderly Big Man had been much further afield than Okapa or Goroka.

As the days passed, I could see more and more clearly his man-between-two-cultures dilemma. One foot marched forward as a "new man" of Papua New Guinea; the other was still planted in the secluded village where he lived with his wife, Ruo, and their infant son, his gardens, his coffee, and his pigs. He was immensely proud, but perhaps too easily willing to reject the traditional ways. His moral judgment about eating rodents was just one lop-sided result of his distant meanderings and cross-cultural experiences.

The daily diet of the Awa is a mixture of both traditional staples and more recently introduced root crops. Old and new blend easily: numerous varieties of sweet potatoes are eaten with the new yellow corn; yams complement cucumbers; ancient *kumu* greens are cooked with peanuts; and traditional *pitpit* shoots consumed with pumpkins created a more diversified diet that was less fully dependent upon the starchy tubers. Our own food ration of one tin of meat per day was supplemented with one or more village-grown vegetables. We always doused the root crops and the monotony of tinned meat with our savored supply of seasonings and spices to alter their blandness, a taste the Awa prefer.

Our imported tins of beef stew, corned beef, or mutton curry were all ordered by mail from the Burns Philp store in Goroka, dropped off by car or plane in or near Okapa, and then carried in with our mail by the runners I sent from Tauna. It was a long and laborious (and probably needless) process to treat ourselves to this minimal meat protein. But more than that, I think these goods symbolized our need to retain contact with the outside world, even if it was just a handwritten note to an impersonal clerk in a grocery store. Gradually, however, our own diet began to change. We relied much more on their healthy abundant vegetables and wild edible plants—pancake-sized, slimy mushrooms, bamboo shoots, and various greens—that grew profusely in the luxuriant rain forest around them.

Cooking was easy to manage by ourselves, but we needed help with the daily household chores of chopping firewood and collecting water. For this we hired Tobi, a smiling, boisterous 16-year-old boy who lived in a small, crowded bachelor hut at Nontorampa, the hamlet where our house was being built. I discovered later that nepotism played a big part in determining who was the best candidate for the job: Tobi was Kawo's younger brother.

I sought out Tobi's help on his first day.

"I want you to go ask some of the women to bring in their vegetables to prepare for our dinner. Not just one or two sweet potatoes as they offered us before, but many of them. Every day we will need food. In return I will give them newspaper (used for rolling cigarettes), salt, or a stick of twist tobacco."

Unlike the children and men, most of the married women did not hang around the hut watching us. They had daily gardening work to do — weeding, clearing, harvesting. None had ever spent a significant amount of time outside the village. Earning money on labor migration, learning to speak Pisin, and participating in the government in Okapa were all men's activities.

Tobi too spoke almost no Pisin, since he was too young to have worked on the coast. What he did learn was picked up from Kawo or some of the other coastal returnees. My Awa was even more rudimentary.

Tobi nodded as if understood and went to seek out some women. Ten minutes later six women sat down on the ground in front of the opening to the hut. I was surprised at the quickness of their response. All were dressed only in their worn bark skirts, which hung in strips from a band around their waist. A few had safety pins stuck in their ear lobes, but they wore no other jewelry. Their heavy string bags were strapped around their foreheads and hung down to the middle of their backs. Almost on cue, when Tobi muttered to them in Awa, they all pulled out bundles and bundles of scallions — and nothing else. Not wanting to appear unaccommodative and discourage them from bringing any more food in the future, I collected their offerings in a pile and paid them with salt. This failure of communication was my mistake: I had not adequately made a distinction to Tobi between a lot of food and a lot of different *kinds* of food.

For several days we had been waiting anxiously for the return of four cargo carriers we sent into Okapa to pick up food and supplies from Ralph's small trade store. We could usually count on several Tauna men to volunteer. All had been former plantation laborers on the coast: Tutu, a handsome young man who was Ila's brother-in-law; Panuma, the son of Entobu, one of Tauna's most respected Big Men; Konato, the sharply dressed man who was involved in the adultery dispute; and Menua, whom Ila always described as "the long man," not only because of his lanky frame but because of the Awa custom of not uttering the name of the *tambu*, a relative through marriage such as an in-law.

At the end of the third day, the sun as usual dipped behind the mountains, forcing the air to cool quickly. Cooking smoke from the huts began to filter through the grass roofs. Out of nowhere the four figures appeared, two abreast, carrying a metal cargo box the size of a steamer trunk lashed to two poles. I thanked the men and threw back the lid and gaped inside. Seven tins of meat, four bottles of beer, and a quart of rum sat at the bottom of the near-empty box. This bore no resemblance to what we had ordered. Ralph had attached a brief, consoling note: Sorry. I've had problems filling your order. Cheers.

On top of this disappointment, the work on the house stopped completely. The workers claimed to have completely run out of nails. Twice I had sent carriers into Okapa with the sole purpose of replenishing the supplies, but each time they had "problems" and returned empty-handed. The framework of the house stood bare, like a huge, gangly skeleton, and our food supplies were exhausted; there was only one thing to do. We would walk into Okapa ourselves and then catch a government truck to Goroka to stock up on a six-months supply of goods once and for all. I also desperately needed to see a doctor for my persistent stomach cramps and diarrhea. (These were possibly caused from the water, which we drank unboiled directly from the stream. One day I saw pigs defecating near our favorite watering spot.)

Our plan was set. Much of the southern route out of Tauna twisted downhill through hidden, muddy trails. Unlike the time when we walked uphill, this trip caused less suffering of the calf muscles, but our knees felt as if skewers had been inserted into the joints. Each step meant a forward advance that our knees had to brake; otherwise we would have ended up trotting down the mountain at breakneck speed. Once through Kopalupa, the vast rain forest, we approached the end, but to us the beginning, of a dirt vehicular road. Government officials and coffee buyers used this road but it was not always passable, especially during the height of the rainy season. Waist-high grass grew in the center between the tire tracks. From this point it was a gradual ten-mile hike into Okapa. The road was part of the boundary between the South Fore and the Awa. All the way to Okapa, the bamboo and *kunai* huts of the South Fore lay alongside the road, spaced between food gardens and shaded plots of young coffee trees. With the vehicular road, the South Fore had direct access to coffee buyers, stores, schools, and the Okapa station. But the Awa, tucked back in the yet unattainable mountain pockets, had no such easy out.

At the small hospital in Okapa, the resident doctor examined me and handed me a bottle of antacid tablets for my stomach pains. From there we bounced along into Goroka in a truck provided by Peter Broadhurst. We walked over to Steamships and purchased five boxes of food, medicine, and another ten pounds of eightpenny nails. That should have been sufficient for a while. Then it was back to Okapa.

We opted for the third and longest approach into Tauna to avoid the troubles of our previous walks. A rough, stone-layered winding road leaves Okapa and reaches an altitude of 8,000 feet, at which point the rich soil turns into a sticky red clay. Finding cargo carriers in one of the Auyana villages to the north of Tauna presented a problem. I could see no eager volunteers. It seemed that many of the healthy men, knowing of our destination, had suddenly come down with severe headaches or had some important business in their sweet potato gardens.

The Auyana, who lived much closer than the Awa to the vehicular road that radiated out from Okapa, sold more coffee and earned more money. They considered heavy labor like carrying cargo to be unprofitable and beneath their dignity. The only available carriers I could muster up were a ragtag band of moneyless young boys and girls and a few married women. The younger ones led the pack, the cardboard boxes carefully balanced on their bare shoulders. But the carriers would only go so far. They had to be changed three times in as many Auyana villages. It could have been the distance or the fear of sorcery from enemy villages or a combination of both reasons. According to the patrol officer's report, which I read in Okapa, the walk from the red clay road to Auyana country to Tauna should have taken four hours. We finally reached Tauna perspiring and sore after seven hours and were elated to be back.

I kept my nails under close surveillance this time, rationing them out like silver nuggets. Remarkably, the men took only a day and a half to complete the rest of the house. Compared to the dark, cramped *haus kiap* where we spent the first three weeks, our new house was airy, clean, and spacious. While the workers bundled the grass to complete the finishing touches on the roof, Kawo pounded in the last nail. He stepped back, his jaws filled with a large gob of red betel, and grinned from ear to ear. Inside the magnificent two-room structure we added shelves, nails for hangers, and set up our folding vinyl camp beds at the front of the house. But because the back of the house slanted down about a foot lower than the front end, the beds slid like skis across the slick bamboo floor. We had to strap the legs of the bed to the wall posts to prevent riding on our beds in the middle of the night.

That was not the only miscalculation. The finished house stood so high and heavy that the short foundation posts had sunk into the mud. The woven bamboo floor, originally two feet above the ground, sagged with the weight of our cargo and barely cleared ground level. Nor did the mosquitoes, fleas, and rats desert us. Having more room to explore, they seemed to grow in number and persistence.

Despite those minor flaws, the joy of moving into the new house raised my hopes that the real fieldwork would begin. I could also see that the

Nontorampa hamlet with the author's house in center.

villagers were immensely proud of their massive construction. They celebrated the occasion by preparing a *mumu*, an outdoor earth-oven pit heated with stones, which overflowed with multicolored sweet potatoes, yams, taro, *pitpit* shoots, and pumpkins.

"All right! Hurry up! Line up!" Kawo barked, mimicking the *kiap*. Resembling a military review, the men who had worked on the house formed a thirty-foot line in front of the house. (Lining up is a new cultural innovation. Men were trained to do this whenever they received pay or were counted for the census.) I left the payment for the house up to Kawo in case arguments developed that I could not handle or understand. We had previously agreed on a price of U.S. $85. Kawo asked me specifically to pay him in Australian shillings (approximately ten cents U.S. each), rather than paper bills, which the tribesmen distrusted. From the metal patrol box I lifted out a bulky bank bag containing $100 worth of coins.

Holding this wealth in his stocky, muscular arms Kawo cleared his throat and delivered a short speech: "We have finished the house. And now Tewe has paid us. If we work hard, we will always have money. That is good. Now we can party and eat from the *mumu*."

Kawo then distributed the coins very slowly and methodically to each man, handling each shilling piece as if it were a precious morsel of pork meat.

"All right! Now the women! Line up!" He went down the line again, paying each one according to how hard he thought they had worked.

In Okapa I was advised to keep wages for informants, workers, and cargo carriers within "reasonable limits," or else the competition would be too steep and the men wouldn't want to carry cargo (it wasn't a highly prized job as it was) for the government patrols. Privately I presented Kawo with a tip for his excellent services, but I never knew whether he understood the purpose of that gift.

Relieved, but still anxious and impatient, I made a mental count of the major difficulties encountered so far: inadequate supplies, frequent miscommunication, Ila's "lost" bar of soap, the perpetual aggravation of the biting insects and rodents, the pounds of "missing" nails, and the slowness of house building. But my excitement ran high that evening. The collective celebration of the villagers, the steaming food from the *mumu*, and the clear, orange sunset all melded together like a busy seventeenth-century Brueghel painting transplanted to the tropics. I felt a deep, but short-lived sense of satisfaction.

I began to think of myself and the task I set out to accomplish in the months ahead as totally self-serving and exploitive. Did every request have to involve money, force, or bribery?

Our mere presence in this small, hidden village already seemed to have irreversibly affected our lives. In Ila I found a man of unparalleled intelligence, friendliness, and humor. I clearly favored his company over the others. Kawo was sometimes completely friendly toward me and at other times totally aloof. Some Big Men, like Api, with whom I desperately wanted to converse, seemed possibly to have become more withdrawn. I, along with the white patrol officers, coffee buyers, store owners, and other outsiders, represented a world he would never fully accept or comprehend. To each man in Tauna my presence was a symbol of either what he wanted or what he wanted to forget.

"Someone has to kill the wild pigs that have been spoiling the gardens around Antepimpa!" Ila shouted, his familiar green sweatshirt disappearing into the forest. He traveled with only his bow and arrows, which rested lazily against his right shoulder.

"I will be back soon. Sometime in the afternoon . . . but maybe not until night." Resigned to his absence, I offered a feeble wave.

I had been trying desperately to get Ila motivated to discuss the genealogies of his kinsmen as a preliminary start to my study of Tauna Awa social organization. But his major preoccupation—I should say total dedication—was directed toward hunting the wild pigs that roamed the surrounding rain forest. Every time I needed him for some work, he seemed to be gone. Little Ausi or Aborate, our next-door neighbors, would usually point to the rugged hills in the north whenever I mentioned Ila's name. I tried to accommodate his interests and gain some insight into hunting techniques at the same time by buying a bow and some arrows from him with the promise that he would teach me how to use them. That tactic never worked out.

Awa men construct their own sturdy six-foot bows from the plentiful black palm tree. First, they cut rough sections of wood into the appropriate lengths, smooth them with an ax or a knife, and then hang them from the rafters of their huts. There, after several weeks, the smoke from the center hearth covers the wood with a rich black finish. Later the ends of the bow are fastened with twine, and a bow string, a quarter-inch-wide strap of flexible bamboo, is attached. These bows are coveted for their craftsmanship throughout the area and in the past were traded to the adjacent Fore and Auyana peoples for shells and feathers. But now the acceptance of Western currency and trade stores had destroyed those traditional patterns of gift exchange.

One event, however, overshadowed the importance of pig hunting and bow making: the upcoming local elections. The offices of councillor and committeeman were to be put up for a new vote. Every day the men sat in a circle in front of the men's hut, gossiping and smoking. Most of them agreed that Abate, the present councillor, the elderly Big Man from Tawaina village, lacked the effectiveness to be a new-style political leader. There was no doubt that he was one of the fiercest Awa warriors before direct colonial influence, only a generation earlier. But now he and many older people failed to adjust to—or plainly rejected—all of the rapid changes occurring around them. Abate had never worked outside the village on European plantations like many of the younger men. He could not quite mentally commute between his view of traditional village life and the new Papua New Guinea of council meetings, road building, coffee growing, and development. His biggest shortcoming, however, was neither his age nor his lack of outside experience: he could not speak Tok Pisin.

The monthly meeting of the Okapa Local Government Council brought together village councillors and committeemen from all the diverse language groups in the District: the Awa, Auyana, North Fore, South Fore, Gimi, Kamano, Keiagana, and Jate. Tok Pisin was the only shared communicative link among all these languages.

For his three years in office the old councillor faithfully trudged up and down mountains to Okapa every month. Kawo, being the committeeman, followed his every step, but he often complained to me that Abate never once spoke up at the meetings. Furthermore, when he returned to the village, he never discussed what had been talked about. I detected some political aspirations on Kawo's part.

The men gathered openly in the hamlet of Obepimpa, collecting the last warmth of the afternoon sunlight. Squatting and smoking, their discussion turned to who should run for office and how the voting would

Tenta stringing a new bow.

turn out. Seizing this opportunity, Kawo stood up and began his informal speech.

"Listen. Listen everyone. We need a new councillor. Everyone knows that. I am the best man for that job. I can speak Pisin, and I understand what the *kiap* means when he talks about development. It means roads, coffee, schools, and plenty of money for everyone. I go to the meetings every month and hear his talk. The white man has big houses and trucks because he has money. If you listen to me, we can get that money too!"

The younger men puffed on their cigarettes of newspaper and tobacco and nodded in approval. The older men, in a cultural quandary, sat back with no sign of emotion on their faces. They silently sucked the smoke from their old, foot-long bamboo pipes. They were being asked to work harder and change a way of life they were quite content with. Would it not bring them shame as men, as warriors, to completely give up their past?

The two subordinate positions of committeeman were also up for a vote, and Ila entered his name in the running. The cadre of men guessed, quite predictably, that each of the three villages would probably vote for its own resident candidate. Both Ilakia and Tawaina villages, numbering about 250 each, offered their own man. Tauna village had the smallest population, so it was not certain whether either Kawo or Ila had a chance at all in the election.

Somewhere from the middle of the dense rain forest that encircled the cleared hamlet areas, urgent shouting broke into a somber meeting. The name of the hamlet was being called.

"Obepimpa-ro! Obepimpa-rooo! We have just wounded a female pig in the back right leg. She is heading west. Come quickly to help us track her down. Obepimpa-rooo!"

I recognized Ila's voice.

Like an impromptu posse in a Western movie, the men abandoned all talk of politics, jumped to their feet with the bows and arrows already in hand, and sped into the bush. Because I knew I could not keep up with their walking pace, much less their running, I stayed behind, feeling like an incompetent child, not quite a man in their culture.

In the evening Ila, head of the hunting party, came to fulfill his duties as my informant. "The pig got away," he said, "but I have two broken arrows to show you. Here, take a look."

I nodded and set them aside, deliberately acting uninterested. "Let's start again with the village genealogies," I suggested. I wanted to determine which clans arrived first, how the men and women were related, where the wives from the outside villages came from, and how villages formed larger alliances through ties of marriage. We began slowly and methodically, but soon my tedious questions about Ila's father, and his father's brothers, and their wives, and their wives' brothers began to bore him. This knowledge was so elementary, so self-evident. Ila abruptly changed the subject of the interview.

"I want to sing a very old song for you," he announced loudly. That caught me off guard. "This is a song from the time before the white man. Be sure to keep the machine on so that I can hear it again and make sure it is right." He pointed to the tape recorder on the table and could tell when it was on by looking at the spinning reels. Not wanting to forego the possibility of collecting any information at all, I relented.

"Oh-oh-oh. Ah-ah-ah-ah. Oh-oh-oh . . ." Ila began his repetitious atonal chant.

Outside I could hear a group of whispering voices. After Ila finished each song the eavesdroppers yelled and shouted with exaggerated gusto so that they too would have their voices recorded. Finally they could stand the isolation no longer. I had set aside these evening interviews for work, not casual visiting, but they had to come inside. Twenty men, women, and children plopped down on the saggy bamboo floor. Over and over they asked me to play back each song. I did—at full volume. This, of course, brought more and more people into the house, and soon my quiet interviewing session with Ila turned into a raucous singing party.

Each man attempted to outdo the other by seeing who could sing the loudest and the longest. The younger men recited the most prurient folktales they knew, just to see the young girls laugh and blush when they heard them retold by the "machine." My only tactic in the midst of this frenzy was to go along with the crowd until they were worn out from the singing and storytelling. Their capacity for gaiety and ribaldry was much larger than mine, and I could not comprehend very much of what was going on.

They wound down along with my batteries after several hours. One by one, they spilled out of the house back to the warmth of their own huts. Ila, acting like a master of ceremonies, was the last to leave. He seemed pleased with himself. The evening had been enjoyable. When he approached the door, I hinted bluntly, "Well, I think tomorrow would be a good day to learn about your relatives and ancestors."

He exhaled from his omnipresent newspaper-and-tobacco cigarette and said, "Of course, Master. That's what I'm here to do! I am your interpreter!"

The piercing sounds of shouting and laughing from the other side of the bamboo walls interrupted my late morning dozing. Another gathering for a singing party? I stumbled to the door and saw a dozen men and women, including Kawo and Ila, wearing what could best be called costumes.

"Tewe. Take our pictures. We want you to take our pictures," they pleaded. I did not even try to understand what brought on this early morning exuberance; I reached for my camera.

Kawo was strutting around in the traditional Awa garb from before the arrival of the Europeans: a bark skirt, shell-and-feather headdress, a bow and arrow poised in his hand, and a triangular wooden codpiece. A drooping pig's tusk nosepiece dangled from his nasal septum.

Twang. Twang. He snapped the bamboo bow string and spat out a red glob of betel juice on the ground.

"You look great!" I declared. "Like a real fierce Big Man, a true warrior."

Twang. Twang. "Yes. This is the way of my ancestors. They put on all of these ornaments and prepared for warfare. If an enemy saw them, they would be afraid of him just by seeing his magnificent posture and fierceness. But we don't dress like this anymore, of course. Only for celebrations."

Kawo spoke with a glint in his eye, and I could see that he felt good about holding on to something of the traditional ways. Although he saw much of the old life giving way to a dubious "progress," it helped occasionally to resuscitate it in a public masquerade.

Ila was another case. From his three indentured labor trips to Port Moresby and other coastal cities, he had purchased an expensive wardrobe that he would pull out of his trunk for special occasions. His idea of dressing up was putting on a pair of bright blue shorts, a clean white T-shirt, sunglasses, a pair of black shoes and socks, and a Mobil

Dressed for a singing; Ila stooping in foreground.

gas station cap. (I never again saw him wear the cap, shoes and socks, or sunglasses.)

"Where's your costume?" I asked. "You don't look much like a warrior to me."

Ila responded quickly. "I am not a man of the past. Wearing those 'bush' clothes would bring me shame. I am a man of shame. You and the others would see me and think that I was just another bush *kanaka*. No! I am a man of the present!"

These dozen waggish figures and their incongruous outfits made a mockery of both the past and the present. A James Bond 007 belt clasped one man's bark skirt; a discarded ball-point pen punctured another's nasal septum; a young mother wore her zippered dress backward so that her breasts would be free to nurse her baby. Behind these costumes I could clearly see different styles of exhibitory expression and what was accepted or rejected.

Ila stepped to the side looking like a jaded tourist and lit a half-smoked cigarette. Like me, he watched his fellow villagers prance around with a detached fascination. He also kept one eye on me, looking at my reactions.

The picture taking and joking rolled into full swing until Panuma ran down the hill from Obepimpa hamlet to summon Kawo. Panuma pulled him away from the crowd.

"Last night," he whispered seriously, "a man snuck into the hut where Nunuma was sleeping. He tried to rape her, but she screamed and he ran away into the forest."

Hearing any public complaint or misdoing, Kawo, acting as the village committeeman, was the judge and jury. He called for an immediate open-air hearing at Obepimpa. The extemporaneous court drew few interested spectators.

Nunuma was a young, married woman whose husband, Tenta, was away from the village working on a coastal copra plantation. She sat demurely on the ground, her legs tucked to the side. She wore only her bark skirt, which modestly covered her pubic region, and a red store-bought necklace. Like that of the other women, her frizzy hair was cut in a neat one-inch mound around her head. Her arms were crossed over her stomach and supported her full breasts.

"What happened last night?" Kawo asked.

Nunuma looked down at the ground and nodded her head.

"Did you recognize who crawled into your hut?"

"No," Nunuma said quietly.

"Do you want to say anything else?"

Nunuma did not move, and the court ended abruptly.

I had noticed that many of these incidents, these daily troubles, led into investigatory deadends. No final resolutions were made, and not even

Ila as a "new man" of Papua New Guinea.

A Big Man dressed for a singsing.

that much interest was shown about what really happened. Even before the court, as soon as Panuma brought down the news, Ila said to me that the woman was lying. He did not want to waste his time going to the hearing. I was puzzled. Why would she lie? On what basis did Ila make this judgment? Why did Kawo even attempt a hearing?

Kawo and I left Obepimpa and headed back toward our houses in Nontorampa. My skillful, subtle questioning would eventually uncover what really happened, I thought.

"Do you think Nunuma . . . ?"

Loud warning yelps broke into my question. Near the top of the narrow footpath that snakes up to the village of Kawaina, we could see tiny moving figures in the distance. Only white men wore hats and boots. It was a patrol. The *kiaps* from Okapa had arrived to supervise the election for the new councillor and committeemen.

Chapter 4

Courts and Councillors

T he first voting for councillor and committeemen took place in 1966. According to Australian mandate, a new election was to be held every three years. These positions were important. Strong, vocal representation at the Okapa Local Government Council could result in many benefits for individual villages.

Even before the morning mist in Tauna had burned off, the people from Tawaina and Ilakia villages had begun to straggle in. Some were bare; others wrapped themselves in old blankets or towels. The Taunans arrived from their scattered hamlets and joined the others in front of the *haus kiap*. Men greeted old friends, lightly squeezing their hands as in a handshake. The women and children gathered to the side, apart from the men, moving without question. This cleared hilly slope, where we spent our first several weeks, soon bustled with visitors and residents.

Bob, a young, lean, agricultural officer from Okapa, stood up first to address the members of the three assembled villages in Pisin.

"You people have to prepare yourselves for self-government and independence. This means that if you don't want to depend upon Australia, you'll have to develop your economy and grow more coffee. If you want to be a good, strong country and not have people think you are backwards, you must show them that you can stand up on your own two feet. Making money is the most important thing for your country!"

Not too many of the Awa could have understood Bob's brief pep talk. Only a quarter of the men, the returned labor migrants, and none of the women or children had any grasp of Pisin. Even then, they could not fully comprehend notions like *economic development, independence,* and the idea of a new country uniting the hundreds of diverse ethnic and linguistic groups.

55

He tacked on a last point: "If you want more money, you should build a vehicular road from here all the way to Okapa so that a truck can come directly to you and buy your coffee." Kawo, standing close to Bob, translated the talk as well as he could into Awa.

Next Taffy, the *kiap*, the more vocal and aggressive of the two, rose from his wooden folding chair and turned toward the crowd. Wearing his rumpled khaki shorts and shirt, he had set a battered Australian bush hat squarely on his head with the drawstring secured firmly under his chin. His heavy leather walking boots were scuffled and well worn. But Taffy, a short, burly Welshman, did not enjoy these patrols through the back country of the Highlands. He had little patience for the villagers, who he thought were too "bushy" and backward because they did not understand the meaning of voting or the responsibilities of their new political roles. His diatribe, delivered in his lilting Welsh accent, was short and to the point.

"You people are the laziest bloody buggers in the Eastern Highlands. All you think about are your pigs and your stinking sweet potatoes. If you want money and cargo, get off your arses and go to work! Plant some more bloody coffee! Build a bloody road! Do it now!"

Then a deathly silence. The men and women buried their stares in the ground. Their shoulders arched forward and, seeking security, they crossed their hands over their stomachs. Even the people who did not understand Pisin got the message from the tone of his voice. I could see fear and shame on some of their faces, and silent anger on others. Were we not free to do what we wanted before the whites came?

I hoped that the villagers did not identify Jackie and me too strongly with them and thus destroy any future relationships. Never were the divisions of colonial Papua New Guinea made so clear as in those few short seconds: the powerful and powerless, administrative officer and indigene, white and black.

Taffy knew well my attitudes from our discussion the night before and could not quite understand why anthropologists should have such "sentimental" views of the villagers. He considered them simply "rock apes," some lowly creatures on his scale of moral and intellectual development.

Mercifully (though without such intention), Taffy called for the election to get underway. The somberness of the crowd turned to anticipation. A count showed that sixty visitors had arrived from Ilakia village, forty-eight from Tawaina, and 52 represented Tauna. Because of the persistent gossip about incompetence, the old councillor from Tawaina chose not to run again. Kawo offered his name for that office, and Ila entered himself for one of the two positions of committeeman. One by one, each person walked to a sequestered table where he or she whispered the name of their choices to the *kiap* who marked them down on a piece of paper. The voting took a little more than three hours.

Taffy and Bob counted the ballots. For the office of councillor, Kawo and the candidate from Ilakia village had tied. In this event, the *kiap* had the authority to appoint the winner. Taffy chose Kawo. (I seriously wondered whether our presence in Tauna had anything to do with this.) Ila won the office of committeeman hands down, and a man from Ilakia took the other position. Hearing the final results, the villagers began to disperse.

Taffy and Bob followed me down to the house, where Jackie was preparing a dinner of fried yams and tinned beef curry. The four of us talked and argued about Papua New Guinea politics and the "ways" of the people until past midnight, when the last fires in the adjacent huts had turned to dim glowing embers, and everyone had fallen asleep.

Despite our irreconcilable differences, I liked Taffy. He was a tough, hard-drinking man, a rugged individualist whom the hills of Papua New Guinea attracted by offering exotic outdoor adventures and good pay. Taffy waddled out of the house and apologized: "Well, you won't be seeing us for at least another year. I guess both of us'll be relieved." He punctuated his comment with a devious chuckle.

At daylight Taffy and Bob waited impatiently for the Tauna volunteers to lug their cargo to Ilasa, a village of Fore people, a day's walk to the south over extremely rugged terrain.

"Get up here, you bloody buggers! Hurry up!" Taffy yelled repeatedly. No one responded.

Finally, Yagai, the policeman from Okapa, managed to round up a bone crew of ten men. Taffy instructed Ila to remember the names of all the men who hid from the patrol. These men, he threatened, would later be sent to jail. Both Kawo and Ila pleaded that they had to attend to the court cases in the village, and they now had earned greater government responsibilities. It was no use. They too had to carry the *kiap's* cargo.

The carriers returned to Tauna the following afternoon, tired and angry. Taffy had paid them only $1.20 each for their back-breaking labor. He had beaten two of the men for dropping a metal patrol box, which they eventually recovered, into one of the fast-swirling rivers. The men pointed to their raw shoulders and hands and asked for medicine. They all complained about the torturous trail to Ilasa and the temperamental *kiap* whom they feared so much.

Several years later, Taffy visited us in Los Angeles while he was on vacation from his duties as a patrol officer. From Los Angeles he planned to fly to Wales, around Europe and Asia, and then back to Papua New Guinea for another two years. A few months after he returned to his job, we learned that on one of the Highland patrols he had accidentally fallen into a river and drowned. His body was never recovered.

The elections were over, and the patrol had left. The village's attention turned to the recent dispute surrounding Aisara, a young, dark, and attractive unmarried woman of twenty and her illegitimate baby.

According to the gossip, which even the little children relayed to me, she had been involved in numerous sexual affairs going back several years. They were mainly with Kawo and one of his clan brothers, Tenta. Both were already married: Kawo to Tewaka, and Tenta, who was working on a coastal plantation, to Nunuma. The problem was neither Aisara's out-of-wedlock child nor her public sexual escapades. The Awa were polygynous, and both men wanted to take her for a second wife.

Wepala, Aisara's father, called for a court hearing. Ila presided over the discussions in the open cleared ground at Obepimpa hamlet because Kawo was too involved with the squabble to be impartial.

What marriage would be acceptable to all of the parties concerned? Ila thought that the marriage would cause too much friction and jealousy between Aisara and Tewaka, Kawo's first wife. Tewaka agreed but had little to say in the matter, for Awa men were the main decision makers in matters of marriage. Nor did Nunuma want to share Tenta with a co-wife. Ila disagreed with both marriages on other grounds. "One wife is enough, just like the white man," he told me petulantly.

Three afternoon court hearings in the open hamlet finished inconclusively. Further discussion had to wait for Kawo, who was attending to council matters in Okapa.

When Kawo returned, the hearings, which turned more and more into a contest of insults hurled between potential in-laws, reassembled to a large gathering. Until then, Wepala, Aisara's patient father, had not been very outspoken. He sat on the side of the hamlet slope weighing all of the comments. Ila prodded him for his opinion. Wepala rose from his crouching position in a single smooth standing movement. He wore only his torn black shorts. Like most of the men, he was short and had wiry arms and legs whose strength was hidden. His unwashed skin was covered with nicks and scars.

"My daughter has a small child and no husband. I have shame over this. It is better that she is married, and I have a son-in-law to give me gifts and money. But look at Tenta. He is already married and does not need another wife. He is not even here."

Wepala turned toward where Kawo was sitting. "You do not have a sister or a female relative of marriageable age to return to my clan. You have no right to marry my daughter. You cannot pay back your debt of marriage, and you, too, are already married."

"I have enough money and goods to pay you and your clan plenty of bridewealth," Kawo shot back. "That is enough! You cannot ask for anymore!"

Wepala was truly disgusted with Kawo's brashness. He jumped to his feet, grabbed his bow and arrows, and bolted over the short hamlet fence.

Kawo called to Wepala's disappearing back and put in the last word. "You are wrong. I am the councillor now. You should listen to me. I will talk to the number one *kiap* in Okapa, and he will agree with me!'' This rift between Kawo and Wepala postponed the public hearings indefinitely.

My structured genealogical interviewing proceeded quite slowly, but these court sessions or public arguments helped me immensely. Keeping detailed records of current disputes and alignments, I could see the obligations of kinsmen, not on an abstract genealogical chart, but how they worked in everyday life.

It was not uncommon, I discovered, for local village councillors and committeemen to pull rank, to take advantage of the new political authority that they thought they had. Kawo and Ila were no different. Without the force of bows and arrows, they still swaggered and bullied people in the same style as the village Big Men did before the whites' arrival. Once Kawo, for example, assembled the villagers together on his return from Okapa, ostensibly to deliver a message about growing coffee. But invoking the law of the *kiap*, he instead ordered them to build him a new cook house, hinting at dire consequences if they did not. It was finished within a week.

But in spite of all the threats, neither Kawo nor Ila seemed to follow through with any real punitive action. The next time I talked to Ila, he caught me completely by surprise.

''I am going to walk up to Tawaina village,'' he said, ''and round up the four women who hid from the *kiap* during their census patrol. I will bring them to court in Okapa. This is not like before, when people had to be afraid of the white man. That was the fashion of our ancestors. These women, these backward people, must be taught a lesson and listen to Kawo and me and the *kiap*.''

''Sure,'' I said sardonically. Ila might have had good intentions, I thought, but it was probably a bluff, another bit of empty talk leading nowhere.

The next morning, the first smoke from the cooking fires came from Ila's hut. Later, when he passed by, Jackie and I were sitting together, trying to warm ourselves in the sun.

''I'll be back by noon to do some work for you,'' he said abruptly, heading toward the Tawaina trail.

I was beginning to adjust to Awa time and didn't get my hopes up that he would return at noon. Just before getting into bed, some fourteen hours later, I heard his Pisin greeting.

''*Gut nait!*'' I peeked out the door. Completely amazed, I saw the four women he sought standing behind him, shy and embarrassed. So were two Tawaina men who acted as their escorts; for to the Awa, allowing women to walk to distant villages unprotected would surely cause more trouble.

The following day, Peter Broadhurst from the Okapa station sent a message to all the villages in the district. All the newly-elected councillors were to come in for a talk about what he wanted them to accomplish during their terms in office. The announcement passed by word-of-mouth from man to man and village to village. Kawo planned to attend this meeting and at the same time escort the Tawaina women to the court in Okapa. Ila was to stay behind to look after the village.

But it was not to be this easy. The Tawainans were not pleased at all with either Ila or Kawo's conduct. Although Tauna and Tawaina shared many ties of friendship, old enmities from past disputes were not totally forgotten. This trouble with the runaways from the census had happened almost every year. Why were Ila and Kawo picking on Tawaina now?

Ila explained it derisively. "Those Tawainans are really bushy people," he said. "They are backward and stubborn and think only of the old ways. They are not like most of us in Tauna. We listen to the *kiap* all of the time. That is the new law. We line up for the census and carry his cargo whenever he wants us to. The Tawainans must be taught a lesson." Kawo agreed.

Judgments of backwardness and bushiness, however, were entirely in the eyes of the beholder. The tribesmen usually used these terms to insult one another. The wealthier Fore and Auyana people considered all of the Awa, including Kawo and Ila, to be the bushy ones. These groups, in turn, were looked down on by other people who worked on government patrol stations or in the towns. The derogations of backwardness continued down the line.

Kawo began to organize the four women for the day-long walk into Okapa when three tough-looking men from Tawaina joined the women and their escorts. They had been sent by an elderly Big Man of the women's clan. The men bounded into Kawo's hut completely unannounced and made themselves at home on the dirt floor. Each man wore a strong bag across his back and held his bow and arrows securely. The leader, a scruffy, unshaven middle-aged man with unshorn ringlets of hair, addressed Kawo.

"The Big Man is afraid that the women will be thrown in jail with no food, and the guards will rape them. He does not want you to take them to Okapa. There will be trouble if you do."

Kawo turned the core of a roasting sweet potato and thought to himself for a long time. He did not want to cause more antagonism between the villages, and he had an obligation of friendship to the former councillor who lived there.

"All right," he said quietly. "But," he added, "I must still go to Okapa and report to the *kiap* what happened. I don't want him to be mad at me."

The Tawaina party felt a victory. They shook hands with Kawo and left quickly for their own village.

Kawo never really made up his mind what to do. Before setting off to Okapa by himself, he pondered about the long hike and stalled for time by shelling some coffee beans. Suddenly, urgent cries echoed down the hills from Yorampa hamlet and broke his concentration.

"Kawi-o. Kawi-o. Kawi-ooo. Come up here quickly. It is very important. Someone has done something against the law. We want you to hold a court. Kawi-ooo . . ."

This time it was reported that Toa, a teenage boy, had attempted to sexually molest a little girl. When Kawo and Ila heard the sketchy details, they agreed that this was of sufficient importance for both of them to walk into Okapa the next day. Kawo asked me to write a letter to Peter outlining the nature of the sexual offense and listing the names of the stubborn Tawaina "bigheads" who wanted no part of the Okapa judicial process. This would make his complaints "official."

The timing of activities in Tauna seemed to fall together in clumps. No one ever just went somewhere to do one thing. Kawo's court cases stirred up the idea among others of also going to Okapa. Several men wanted to carry Mota, a feeble crippled boy, to the hospital. On the way, some of them planned to sell some coffee beans or their handcrafted bows to the Fore and shop at the trade store. One thing led to another; that was the key to their multipurpose travel.

Now full-blown, the bulky party of twenty left at noon with plans to sleep down near the Lamari River in some temporary shelters and then walk to Okapa the day after. I was angry that Ila had joined the group, especially because of my slow progress on the village genealogies. He promised in his usual manner, "Of course, I'll be back soon. I have work to do for you!"

My attention turned to the more mundane matters of vegetable gardening and redigging deeper ditches around the house in order to keep the heavy rain from muddying the narrow footpath between the main house and the cook house. Steps away, the old women and naked children quietly prepared their evening meal of bright orange yams and kumu greens. They guessed that Kawo and Ila would return in three days. How they arrived at that conclusion, I never knew; but they were wrong. For once Kawo and Ila showed up *ahead* of everyone's estimates. Less than twenty-four hours had passed when they strode back into the village accompanied by a determined policeman from Okapa.

Kawo, Ila, and the policeman stopped only to eat and rest for a short while. Ila told me that Toa was reprimanded in Okapa for his attack on the young girl, but no other punishment had been meted out. The law-abiding gang of three finished eating and continued straight up to Tawaina, again to round up the four elusive women who avoided the census. Two of them were easy to track down. The other pair had to be chased through the rain forest and handcuffed. The entire crew marched back to Tauna in single file while it was barely light. They left for Okapa once again at daybreak.

Ila offered me his assurance that he would be back the following day. "Sure, this other work is what I have to do as the committeeman. But the work for you is real work. It's work for money!"

I was disheartened, but of course I had no right to interfere with his new duties. I considered training a new key informant, but it seemed that no one else in the village had the ability for this daily, detailed, tedious ethnographic interviewing. I knew that Ila was absolutely the best possible informant. In just a few months he had taught me far more about interviewing, field methods, and ethnography than I had ever learned in a university. He would remind me to turn on the tape recorder when he had an interesting story to tell, important gossip from another village, or a new village place name or ancestor I had not yet recorded in my genealogies.

He would often say, "I don't want to keep reminding you of these things and repeat myself. Put them on the machine so that you won't forget!"

He knew exactly which data I had collected so far and could fill in holes that I forgot and correct my mistakes. Often, when interviewing older, monolingual Awa informants, he took the initiative in asking them questions about warfare and the migration of people, always anticipating my next question and sometimes asking his own. We usually talked inside my house at night, illuminated only by the flicker of a single candle. It is difficult to convey in words the highs of suddenly seeing the parts of another culture's puzzle mesh together.

I had fantasies of holding Ila hostage and working together with him for a year, free of all distractions, in some isolated hotel room somewhere. I could not wait until he returned from Okapa. I had so many new questions to ask.

Panuma, chewing on a large wad of betel, stepped into the house and cruelly interrupted my daydream. He had just walked back from Okapa with our mail.

"The court won't be held for another three or four days, maybe even a week or longer," he reported. "Ila and Kawo and the rest of them will stay there until then."

Since the first Australian patrols explored the Awa area in the early 1950s, money, first gradually and then fully, became incorporated into the village economy. This economic colonialism eventually meant the death of most traditional values and forms of wealth. Awa dependency on the local trade store, distant labor markets, and ultimately the international market had been made complete. It was not law and force that pacified the truculent tribesmen; it was tins of mackerel and gaudy trinkets.

The Taunans now persistently pestered me to buy many of their now-devalued traditional artifacts. As far as I knew, I gave them little or no encouragement, but they came into the house anyway with their bows and arrows, carved wooden headrests, woven string bags, drums, shell necklaces, and feather headdresses—all as a way to acquire money. I bought a few items just to be accommodating, and with the few dollars I paid them they would take the money and spend it on cheap shorts or dresses, tinned fish and meat, or brightly colored, perfumes, odiferous to my nose, not to theirs. A more symbolic loss could be noted here: they were actually selling off the old traditions, something for which a precise value could not be attached, at rock-bottom prices.

Short of funds myself, I was reluctant to purchase any artifacts just to help them, and least of all to show off as souvenirs of fieldwork when I was back in the United States. I also didn't want to start a stampede into the house and have it known that it had turned into a kind of trading post. Already several men and women from the more distant villages had walked for a day or more to offer me their aged possessions, most of which were so filthy and decrepit that they didn't want them themselves. I saw the strategy they were using. Trying to sell me a faded, torn string bag or a few broken arrows was a final move before these goods were relegated to a dump heap in a dark corner of their huts.

Money also seemed to be one of the most important (but not the only) reason why many younger men in the village—sometimes as much as half of the adult male population—willingly signed up for indentured labor stints on the coastal plantations of Papua New Guinea. There they would toil for two years, chopping coconuts or tapping rubber for not much more than pocket change. A current rumor in the air was that several younger teenage boys would soon be on their way to Okapa and then Goroka to join some of the other Awa men who were already on the coast. They were following in the footsteps of what Ila, Kawo, and some of the other men had done for the first time a decade earlier.

More than seeing us as wealthy collectors of artifacts, the villagers also sought us for our presumed medical expertise. But other than common sense and a slight knowledge of first aid, neither Jackie nor I had any practical medical training. That did not stop people from staggering into the house or pounding on the door at all hours of the day and night with deep, bloody lacerations or milder complaints, such as a month-old scratch on the thigh or sometimes a completely feigned ailment. One sick or wounded person usually attracted the attention of another who remembered a scratch he incurred several weeks ago, and so this went on to the next "patient." Even the smallest toddlers joined in the rush to receive the benefits of modern medicine. One by one they begged me to daub their dried-up sores with gentian violet and cover them with a new "flesh-colored" bandage (which was about ten shades lighter than their flesh).

My defense against these round-the-clock troubles was to limit "visiting hours" to a one-hour time period in the morning. Otherwise,

I would not have been able to do any kind of work on my own. We made exceptions, of course, for serious wounds and ailments like pus-filled ulcers and severe cuts on the limbs, but we had no efficient way to treat these wounds. Our medical kit was disastrously incomplete. Jackie and I could only treat the ill with antiseptic, give them aspirin or a malaria tablet, or suggest that they attempt the long walk to the small hospital in Okapa.

I tried to discover the most important health problems of the villagers and began keeping a detailed chart of those who requested medical help and the reasons for their visit. Their ideas of illness and its causes, however, were not as obvious as Western epidemiology might suggest. Awa well-being was tied intimately to beliefs about ghost attacks, malevolent spirits who lived in the forest, prophetic dreams, food taboos, and sex-role behavior. It was this complex cosmological interrelationship that I had to unravel before I could even begin to understand something as apparently simple as the reasons for a headache.

The government had also repeatedly made suggestions to improve village sanitation by telling the Taunans to live in one or two large hamlets, rather than seven scattered ones, and keep the domestic pigs and pit latrines away from the areas for eating, sleeping, and bathing. When Kawo and Ila returned from Okapa, after a week, they were beginning to feel that the law in Okapa, while powerful, was too distant and too busy to deal with local troubles. In court, the four scared women from Tawaina were told simply to show up for any future census counts and were let go.

Kawo and Ila were sure that they could get away with taking the law into their own hands as long as they recited the fearsome litany that "the *kiap* told us to do it." The older men and women suffered the most. They did not understand the need for the burdensome, sometimes petty rules that were imposed on their daily lives and challenged the traditions of their ancestors. Because all of the villagers were expected to be obeisant and unpresupposing in front of the *kiap*, they directed much of their frustration at Kawo and Ila, warning them that they should not interfere with the "old ways" as much as they were doing.

Kawo tried in a positive way to breach the generation gap and create a greater sense of village unity. He did this by attempting to convince the others to participate with him in the upcoming Goroka *singsing*. This was a large, annual festival of singing and dancing that attracted hundreds of tourists from all over the world. Colorful, painted tribesmen from every corner of the Highlands were garbed in elaborate traditional costumes and assembled for the week-long festivities in the Goroka showgrounds. From the tourists' point of view, this show presented an unforgettable melange of colors, sights, and sounds that could not be seen anywhere else in the world. My stay with the Awa, however, forced me to see it from another perspective: as an inauthentic, showy, stage production in which Highlands "natives" could play at and portray "primitive" and "savage" warriors for tourist cameras.

Later that week, Kawo walked up to Tawaina village to try to persuade them to join him in Goroka. Repeating the phrases of the kiap, he wanted to make sure that the people of the Okapa District would be well represented. I trailed along.

Kawo swaggered in his characteristic bowlegged gait and approached a group of men who were sitting lazily and smoking around the entrance to the men's hut. They were obviously enjoying their uninterrupted moment of peaceful relaxation. The reception was cool. Some of the men were still miffed about Kawo's handling of the Tawaina runaways. Without looking up, they offered their hands to greet Kawo and me. Kawo touched each of them in turn and began to describe the purpose of his visit. Using a loud, persuasive tone of voice, he sounded deliberately like a kiap.

"Everyone must go to the singsing. We have to show the head kiap and the rest of the people around Okapa and Goroka that we are as good as them. We should think about the finery and decorations that we will wear. We don't want to be rubbish men or men of shame!"

Still silent, the men nodded in agreement, a nod that indicated that they were listening rather than agreeing. Kawo got the message and cut short his speech. The dead, hot afternoon air had slowed him down, too.

Kawo and I hopped back down the trail toward Tauna with a sense of total futility. Ten minutes passed in silence before he turned to me and said, "Those Tawaina bigheads are just a bunch of bush kanakas. All they think about are their pigs and sweet potatoes."

Hearing of the plans for the Goroka singsing, three men from an Auyana village to the north came down to visit Ila in Tauna. They were crouching and smoking in his cool, dark hut when Kawo and I returned. My first thought was to try to interview them about their kinship relationships with Tauna men. I needed an interpreter to do this. Kawo had already walked off toward one of his gardens. I looked around everywhere for Ila, when one of his unattended guests mumbled something about pig hunting. At that moment, I saw Ila, bow and arrow in hand, head toward us. He knew exactly what was on my mind; and I knew what was on his. Before I could even speak, he opened his mouth, "First I have to cut some bamboo irrigation tubes for my taro garden, and then I'll be right back. You wait a while." He shook hands perfunctorily with his Auyana visitors and then zipped up a small footpath.

Ila returned many hours later, and the Auyana men had since gone. I was terribly frustrated with him but kept back my emotions. I decided to try a new tactic. A public show of force and power seemed to be what the Awa responded to the most. Their own leaders, including Ila, organized men and work tasks in much the same way. Yelling, gesturing, and commanding was what I had to do.

Ila was in sight thirty feet away when I talked toward him and raised my voice. "You're always lying to me. You promise me you'll be here when you're out pig hunting or giving some other excuse. If that's how you want it, fine! I'll find myself another informant!" I turned abruptly and strode into my house, hoping secretly that this bluff would work and Ila would begin to take his informant duties more seriously.

Early the next day, just as the morning sun climbed over the lowest hills, I heard a sound at the door. Tap. Tap. Tap. "Are you Up?" Tap. Tap.

I pulled myself out of the cot and saw Ila standing outside the door chewing on his customary breakfast of raw sugar cane and spitting out the shreds. Large smiles appeared between chews. He wore a clean pair of striped shorts and a fresh, red T-shirt. It was neither his pig-hunting nor his gardening outfit.

"Good morning," he said cheerfully. "How about doing some work now?"

Only half-awake, I did not turn down his offer. Appearing to be put upon, I was of course immensely pleased—almost ecstatic—that he came to work on his own initiative. I sat down at my small folding card table and hurriedly reviewed my notes and questions on village genealogies. We went back and forth over the material for almost two hours. Then I could sense Ila's interest began to wane and called for a break.

That was the best session I had had so far, and the information could keep me going for several days. I saw many inconsistencies in my notes. Sometimes informants gave two or three names for themselves and others. The Awa also followed a taboo on uttering the name of in-laws. This proscription, known as teknonymy, is found in many cultures around the world. Ila, for example, had to address and refer to Tintau, his father-in-law, indirectly, as the "father of Ruo" or the "husband of the short woman who lives at Yorampa hamlet."

I was getting a clearer idea of the spatial and social organization of the five major patrilineal kinship groups in the village. Each named group lived in its own hamlet area; each group owned specific land plots around the village; and each group was exogamous, that is, men and women had to find a spouse from outside their natal kinship group.

These kinship groups were the basis of the social organization of the village. These kin groups, or clans, were also divided into smaller units of lineages and sublineages. A person normally acquired clan membership from his or her father; thus, in the anthropologist's jargon, they were referred to as patrilineal descent groups.

Related men,—for example, brothers, fathers, uncles (on the father's side) and (patrilateral parallel) cousins—tend to stay put. They live in the same hamlet and plant their gardens on nearby clan-owned land.

Tauna Awa Kin Groups

Major Kin Groups (Clans)	Minor Kin Groups (Lineages)
Tanuna	Tamiopina
	Machampa
	Abampa
	Unnamed units
Aramona	Anewerampa
	Tumerapa
	Imiana
	Po'nia
	Unnamed units
Obepina	Alaula
	Paranorarapa
	Unnamed units
Apia (or	
Nonakia)	Unnamed units
Awatera	Unnamed units

Females, on the other hand, live in their father's hamlet until they are married, at which time they reside in their husband's hamlet with his clan group.

Ideally, that's the way the system worked, but in actual practice there were many exceptions to the rules of kin-group membership, which land people used for gardens, and where they lived before and after marriage. Only the rule of clan exogamy had no exceptions as far as I could determine.

Spatially, the unity called Tauna village was actually made up of seven separated hamlets. Hamlets are cleared areas in the grassland or forest that are surrounded by a five-foot-high slat fence. They all had names, so that a person could say that his house was in Nontorampa (the hamlet where our house was built) or Yorampa or Wenipa.

Each hamlet had six to a dozen usually round windowless huts made of grass roofing and bamboo sidewalls. Teenage boys and married men slept in a men's hut. Married women slept with their children. An isolated menstrual hut was used during their monthly periods and for childbirth. Every hut included a center hearth for cooking and warmth. People slept either on grass mats, a blanket on the ground, or on bamboo beds.

A SAMPLE GENEALOGY:
Ila (Apia clan) and some of his closest kin*

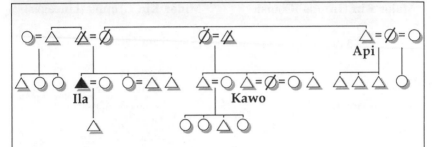

> * Most of Ila's patrilineal relatives (i.e., his father's brother's children) live
> in the Auyana village of Waipina. Api (Tanuna clan) is Ila's mother's brother;
> Kawo (Obepina clan) is Ila's mother's sister's son.

All of the land around the village, not just the hamlets, had a name, whether it was a new or disused garden, a grove of bamboo trees, dense primary forest, or hilly grassland. Walking a hundred yards, one could pass through a dozen different, named parcels of land, like city blocks. Tauna had virtually no level land: as soon as you took a step, you were either walking uphill or downhill. A specially shaped tree or a mythic boulder or a patch of flowers marked the transition from one zone, which I could not see unless it was pointed out to me, to the other. For example, Antepimpa was a high-elevation, heavily forested part of the village. Ururampa was Ila's coffee garden; Wopimpa was a bamboo forest where ghosts and malevolent spirits dwelt. I collected over 500 names of sections of the village from Ila, who knew the clan ownership, mythic significance, and cultivation history of each one.

Much to my surprise Ila came back for another two hours in the afternoon, and again later in the evening. My forcefulness, I thought, had paid off well.

The next day the clan at Nontorampa hamlet prepared an outdoor *mumu* oven. While the people gathered to eat, Ila and Kawo planned to present their talk about participating in the big Goroka *singsing*.

"Come with us to Goroka," Kawo shouted. "We will show everyone how much wealth we have and how fine our decorations are."

The response was lukewarm. The women busied themselves by skinning the foot-long yams and sweet potatoes. The older men sat around the open pit smoking their bamboo pipes and yawning. Children crouched by their mothers or chased each other, shooting miniature reed arrows from tiny bows.

Women preparing food for an earth oven.

Piling dirt and leaves on an outdoor oven.

Ila took over. He shifted his balance and started the verbal assault.

"Everyone around us—the Fore and Auyana—has plenty of wealth. They work hard. They grow more coffee. Next time I go to the council meeting in Okapa with Kawo, I will tell the *kiap* that we are ready to build a road through the village. If we have a road, trucks can come through and buy our coffee. I will tell the *kiap* that we want a hospital here and a school for our children who don't do anything all day and a police station where the *haus kiap* stands. I will tell him we want all the new ways of the government!"

Ila caught his breath and continued. "The Fore and Auyana will go to the *singsing* in their finest costumes—feathers, mother-of-pearl shells, *kapul* skins. We can't let them beat us. We have to show the *kiap* our strength!"

Ila's oratory dissipated into the air along with the steam from the *mumu*. A few men nodded politely, but most of the villagers, including Ila's wife, Ruo, went about their business. Knowing the difficulties of organizing any kind of joint project, I was doubtful that much would come of Kawo or Ila's plans. And I was beginning to wonder whether they gave their talks just to act out their government responsibilities or whether they really felt the Goroka show was that important to their pride.

The day before leaving for Okapa, and then onto Goroka in the back of government pickup trucks, Ila and Bokis, his precious hunting dog, a brown, scrawny, underfed mutt, made one more concerted attempt at pig hunting. They rose in the dark even before the crow of the roosters and left for the dense rain forest to the north. There the mountains sloped sharply up from the village, forming several jagged peaks over seven thousand feet high. These dense patches of primary-growth rain forest were too tangled and stony for gardening, but this was where the feral pigs roamed freely. When hungry, they would trot toward the Awa gardens at lower elevations, break through the wooden slat fences, and ravage the newly planted shoots of the tubers.

Everyone knew the destructiveness of the wild pigs had to be stopped: it was a matter of food. Freely philosophizing, Ila expressed it quite eloquently: "We don't look after sweet potatoes, the sweet potatoes look after us."

Ila's distant call to the hamlet sliced through the heavy bank of morning mist. "Nontorampa-ro. Nontorampa-roooo. Hurry up! I shot a *kanti* (barbed wooden) arrow. It hit the leg of a large male pig. It is running toward Yamantampa and Api's sweet potato garden."

Kawo and his father-in-law, Konoi, grabbed their bows and arrows as they were swallowing their morning meal of sweet potatoes and rushed ahead of the spot where Ila's voice could be heard. Every few minutes the sound of their chase reverberated back to the hamlet. Finally, success. Four barbed arrows had punctured the huge pig's left side and internal

Ila and a newly killed pig.

organs. Its heavy, bloody body was lashed by its feet to an eight-foot-long pole. The hunters marched into the hamlet like victorious warriors. Children pirouetted around Ila's feet and touched his still-warm prize trophy. They tugged at the six-inch curved tusks that encircled its gaping maw.

Whenever any pig, domestic or wild, was killed, the villagers usually gathered together for a *mumu*. That afternoon, the barbeque-like smoke rose lazily into the air, smelling distinctly of fresh pork. When the men had gathered around, Ila melodramatically told and retold the story of how, where, and when he tracked down the renegade pig and how his success only came about because of Bokis, his invaluable hunting dog.

Several hours had passed, and Ila pulled the mud and leaves from the top of the steaming *mumu*, separating the protective cover from the pyramid of food underneath. One by one he called his clan mates, in-laws, friends, and then Kawo and Konoi, who had helped in the chase. He handed each a section of pork. A large, gristle-covered thigh and leg went to Tintau, his father-in-law, the back to some friends, and the head to still others. Ila also presented a section of leg to us. Jackie ducked into the house and recooked it in a spicy mixture of soy sauce, black pepper, fresh ginger root, and garlic powder.

Overcome with his excitement and exuberance to show his generosity, Ila had left nothing to himself. All of the meat was gone. Jackie and I then decided that he should have our portion back. Out it came from the frying pan dripping in its rich sauce. Ila was touched. "The next pig I kill will go only to you and Kawo. The rest of these people," he added quietly, "are too greedy to give anything in return."

I felt close to Ila, as if we had really shared some new understanding. He bit heartily into the spiced cooked meat and gave a slight grimace. "What happened?" he asked.

The next morning Kawo, Ila, and only three other men left for Okapa and then on to the Goroka show. They had planned to be gone at least a week, maybe even longer. The village immediately quieted down. There were no more *mumus*, no lectures, and no public court cases. In fact, it seemed a bit boring. But their absence gave me the time to work over my field notes and genealogies.

April arrived and with it the bright, blue skies lasted longer in the afternoon, and the rains seemed to subside, sometimes not falling for several days in a row. We had made plans to leave Tauna for a short break at the end of the month. Every anthropologist, missionary, and patrol officer had told us that it was essential for our well-being to leave the village occasionally, preferably at two-month intervals. By doing so, we would gain a wider perspective on what we had done and would keep ourselves from falling into the depression, anxiety, and loneliness that can plague isolated fieldworkers.

Less than three months of fieldwork were tucked under my belt, but I was already beginning to know those feelings well. It seemed that the only verification that we existed came from weeks-old letters from our friends and relatives. What the newspapers and our ragged back issues of *Time* magazine called "current events" described a world with little meaning or direct relevance to the lives of these isolated villagers. They were beginning to have no more meaning to us as well, except as faded reminders of another, faraway world.

One hot, sunny afternoon, Ruo, Ila's shy and gentle wife, who stood barely five feet tall, came by the house with a message. Unlike most of the bare-breasted Awa women, Ruo usually wore, in addition to her bark skirt, a brightly colored, hip-length blouse with puffy shoulders. Ila had bought several of these for her at the trade store. For most of the women around Okapa or the Highlands towns, these blouses, along with full cloth skirts and the occasional store-bought beads, formed their usual daily dress. These coverings, to the Awa, were more a matter of fashion than an acquired taste of Western modesty.

Ruo stood before me bashfully and had to be accompanied by several children just to talk to me at all, even though her hut was less than a hundred feet away. "Ila and Kawo and the others are on their way back from Okapa. They will be here soon," she said slowly in Awa. She repeated the message for my benefit.

How does she know? I asked myself. How does anyone around here get to know the difference between truth and rumor? Was I the only one who was confused?

The evening clouds and darkness had completely covered the valley floor when voices, loud, deliberate voices, outside the house aroused me. I kicked away the wooden doorstep and saw both Kawo and Ila just standing there, grinning. Kawo wore a new pair of shorts and a white, buttoned shirt. Pinned to it was a shiny metallic councillor's badge that he had received in Okapa. I was excited and wanted to ask them about their reactions to seeing the hundreds of other tribesmen and the hordes of foreign tourists in Goroka. Seen from the perspective of this small village, the idea of Goroka, a Highlands town with roads, cars, hotels, supermarkets, and electricity drew an envious but hazy image. It was only 60 air miles away, but it could have been 6,000 miles for all its importance to most of the villagers.

"What happened in Goroka? How was the *singsing*? What did you do?" I blurted out.

"Not much," Ila replied blandly. "We didn't go to Goroka. We stayed in Okapa all this time."

Now I was totally confused. Why didn't people here ever do what they said they were going to do? "Why? What happened?" I pressed again.

"We went to Okapa with Tunumu, the man who lives in the small hamlet above Obepimpa. His baby daughter, Yosepe, was sick with bloody diarrhea. You know her. You gave her some medicine, but it didn't work. The doctor's medicine in Okapa was no good either. She died yesterday. Tunumu wrapped her body in a blanket and carried her back."

Ila simply described the stark facts of death as it occurred. Veterans in the daily battle against illness and death, neither Ila nor Kawo seemed to be visibly saddened. I did not see Tunumu around. He had gone straight back to his house.

The *mumu* held on Nontorampa the following day fulfilled a dual purpose. First was the talk that Kawo wanted to deliver about his meeting with the *kiap* in Okapa and how the government wanted to increase the sales of coffee in the area. This always seemed to be the message. A second reason was the public burial of Yosepe.

Kawo began his speech near the heat and smoke of the earth oven. In order to make his talk more official and authoritative, he recited the entire lecture in Pisin to Ila, who then translated it into Awa. Much of the crowd, as usual, showed little interest at all in the government's plans for development. They had heard this same talk many times before.

Kawo finished speaking and joined a group of men sitting thirty feet away from the women. They huddled in a small circle, discussing Tunumu.

"We should do something," one man said. The others agreed with their eyes.

"Yosepe was Tunumu's second child to die in this rainy season," Kawo broke in. "I know the reason. He lets his pigs sleep in the same hut as his wife and children. The *kiap* said that we would get sick and die if we did this like our ancestors. We must stop this sickness and death."

All of the men nodded and grunted. Kawo outlined a plan, and he and five other men stood up to leave. While Tunumu was still clearing some brush for a new taro garden, the men followed a narrow muddy path to his hut. Kawo carefully removed Tunumu's possessions, and then lit two dry, bamboo torches, which he touched to the grass roof. The flames jumped five feet into the air, capped by a cloud of dense, black smoke. Burning down Tunumu's hut and pig sty meant clearing the air of illness and driving away the malevolent spirits who were always attacking small, vulnerable children.

Tunumu was alerted by the black smoke and ran back toward his hut. He saw the sheets of flame swallowing his hut, and the men, including his own clan brothers, idly observing the spectacle. There was nothing he could say or do. He well knew the reason. Tunumu slumped down on his haunches and closed his eyes.

Chapter 5

The Pumpkin's Nose

Every few months, when enough red coffee berries were picked, washed, and dried, the villagers made preparations for their overnight trip through the rain forest to the vehicular road in South Fore territory. Before leaving, Ila had heard of the small weekly raise we offered Onka, our new household helper who replaced the erratic Tobi. Onka, a slim, dour, unmarried man of twenty, had worked previously on a coastal copra plantation. He was used to the notion of regular working hours. Young Tobi was not.

Early one Sunday, I heard Ila standing outside our house joking loudly and deliberately with the children. That was his way of letting me know that he was awake and available. I knew what he wanted, but I was in no mood to discuss wages with him, and I fell back asleep. Ila joked with the children for another hour before I got up.

"You don't get up early enough in the morning," Ila greeted me. "I always have to wait for you to do any work."

I had no stomach to argue so early in the morning and changed the subject. "When will you be back from selling your coffee?"

"Monday, tomorrow night," he answered. Then a pause. "Ah . . . Onka told me that you gave him . . ."

I cut him short. "I'll think about it. But I have one thing to say before you leave. We aren't working enough. We aren't talking enough. Raises, you know, are for people who work hard, like Onka."

Ila had completely expected that kind of answer, but he simply decided to try me beforehand. If I gave in without an argument, fine. If I didn't, then he knew where he stood.

75

"That is true," he said, agreeable as ever. "I will work for you all day and night on Monday when I and the others return from selling coffee."

On Monday, all day, the rain poured down like never before. Torrential sheets of water relentlessly pounded the ground, creating small streams all around the hamlet. Water blew through the bamboo walls of the house, soaking our beds. Fortunately, I slept through much of it. I had a dream that Ila was the anthropologist and I his informant. This idea was so entertaining that I tried to prolong my sleep in order to find out what had happened.

Quite content in my fantasy, I heard knocking at the door at midnight. It was Onka. He was sleeping in the small men's hut about eighty feet away and had heard distant calls outside the hamlet. He came to get my umbrella and flashlight. I stood up, groggy and grumpy, and aimed the flashlight outside. Water sprayed us from everywhere. In the dim light, I could see two shadowy figures head toward us. I couldn't quite believe what I was seeing. I could see Ila and Kawo approaching. Ila held an umbrella in one hand and a kerosene lamp in the other. Kawo also carried an open umbrella and had wrapped a towel around his head. Neither said anything about the rain or the incredible walk they must have endured.

"The rest of the people decided to sleep down by the river in the temporary shelters," Ila declared. "Kawo and I came back together."

"You two better go and sit by the fire and rest," I said.

"Don't you want to work now?" Ila asked, knowing that I would turn him down.

"No. No. Never mind. Tomorrow," I had to answer.

Not wanting to lose a precious day, Ila took off on a pig hunt and was nowhere in sight by the time I got up the next morning. The sky was bright and clear, and the sun's heat caused the moisture from the rain to steam upward from the ground and the drenched grass roofs. Kawo gnawed on a two-foot piece of sugar cane near his house. He looked dry and serene and none the worst for walking all night in the rainstorm.

I knew that Kawo was extremely busy with chores as the village councillor, but I thought it might help me to use him regularly as an interpreter and informant. Kawo spoke Pisin well but was less comfortable than Ila in formal interviewing sessions. He did not always seem to grasp the nuances of my questions. Much of this, of course, was my fault. Kawo was also not entirely sure whether any outsider, including me, should be trusted, whether in exchanges of information or friendship.

A small earth oven began steaming in the afternoon to cook one of Puwante's small pigs, which a curer had determined was killed by a ghost. A public mumu was the best way to distribute the pieces of pork. I approached Kawo while the pig and vegetables were cooking and called him into the house to speak to him privately. I didn't want another

runaway group singing session, especially with all the mumu visitors
outside. I was particularly interested in the wealth differences between
the older generation of traditional Big Men and the men under thirty-
five, almost all of whom had worked on the coast. What kind of store-
bought goods did each group like to buy? Did the younger men sell more
coffee and buy more clothing and tools? Did they save any money? Did
they have to give some of their earnings to the older men?

I studied a list of questions I had prepared beforehand about each man's
coastal work experiences. Kawo began immediately by talking about his
first airplane ride to Port Moresby. Fifteen minutes later, Ila strolled into
the house with his usual unhurried gait. A ring of thick tobacco smoke
guided his entrance. I nodded to him and left the tape recorder on. Ila
sat cross-legged on the bamboo floor of the study and picked up some
news magazines. He leafed through them, as he had done dozens of times
before, gazing absentmindedly at the colorful advertisements for food
and clothing. Kawo and I continued our subdued conversation at the card
table. A few minutes passed, which seemed more like an hour, and Ila
yawned and walked outside.

I talked with Kawo a little longer, just to prolong a sense of authenticity
in our meeting. Then he, too, began to fidget uneasily and excused himself
to go to the mumu. I felt horrible for making Kawo uncomfortable and
for perhaps alienating Ila in a transparent bid for his cooperation.

I jabbed my fork distractedly at a dinner of mumu vegetables and set
aside the half-eaten plate. Onka grabbed the teapot to boil some water.
That was the unspoken signal that we were done eating. Precisely then,
Ila rushed into the house with speed that I had never seen before, except
when he was tracking a marauding pig.

"I've been waiting for you to finish eating. Now that you're done, let's
go. I'm ready!"

I could barely keep my excitement down. Ila seemed to be fired with
more enthusiasm than ever before. Apologetically, I handed him some
tobacco and a strip of newspaper to patch up any damage between us.
Ila first tended to his cigarette, smoothing it in his palms and licking
the edge with great pleasure. His vocabulary and range of expression were
truly remarkable. He recounted vividly the details of a bloody bow-and-
arrow battle between Tauna and Ilakia villages that took place a decade
earlier. I sat completely spellbound in the dim candlelight for nearly two
hours.

The slew of children always around the house meant a never-ending
supply of informal informants. Often I would question them on the use
of various plants and their names. Even the tiniest four- or five-year-olds
could describe precisely where numerous species of domestic and wild
foods could be found.

Several months earlier, we had planted a pumpkin in our garden, and we watched it mature every day. When it was orange and firm, I cut the stalk from the ropy vine and held it up to admire. It was perfectly symmetrical, the size of a basketball. The children who had been observing me shared my pleasure, and I was beginning to think that I could develop greater approval in their eyes as a competent gardener.

"It will be delicious when you cook it," they all chirped.

I suddenly thought of Halloween. I took a sharp kitchen knife and carefully cut out the seeds and the edible portions and set them aside. Working from the top, I cut out holes for two ears, a mouth with jagged teeth, and a triangular section for the nose. When it was dark, I placed a candle inside the hollow core and the familiar jack-o-lantern face lit up the ground outside the house. I told the children how I had made the "spirit" of the pumpkin come alive. They gazed at it and laughed and wrapped their arms around their own shoulders for comfort.

Just then Kawo walked by. "What do you think this is?" I asked.

"You have made a face in the pumpkin. But it's wrong."

"What do you mean," I asked, slightly deflated.

"Noses have two holes. See," he said, pointing to his own. "Not just one big hole like you made."

Lately, Kawo had little time to stop and chat. He was either coming or going somewhere in a hurry. He had also been preoccupied because of his wife's pregnancy. She was almost due, and he wanted very much to have a son. Tewaka's two earlier pregnancies had ended in stillbirths.

One evening Tewaka walked quickly past our house. She was dressed only in a bark skirt, which swished with every graceful step, and a swatch of store-bought cloth which covered one shoulder and her bulging belly. Her breasts were full; her nipples and areolae had become widened dark circles. She offered a friendly smile. Ayato, an older woman and the experienced mother of five children, accompanied her to the special menstrual hut. The menstrual hut sat just thirty feet behind our house, at the far end of the vegetable garden. No men, of course, were allowed anywhere nearer it, for the Awa believe that male contact with women in these states could lead to illness or possibly even death.

Sometime in the middle of the night I heard the screams and cries of childbirth. But since the menstrual hut was off limits to me as a male, I turned over and fell back asleep. Everything probably went smoothly because no one came to fetch Jackie for medicine. The morning brought the news. Tewaka had given birth to a baby girl. The afterbirth and blood would have to be buried in the ground of the menstrual hut, and Tewaka would nurse the baby until both of them were strong. The older, knowledgeable women of the village would see to Tewaka's food and other needs. Kawo was to stay away until several weeks passed, and his wife and daughter could leave the menstrual hut.

Kawo organized a mumu later that day in the hamlet to mark the birth of his first child. The turnout, however, was sparse. Kawo was greatly offended that most of the clansmen from the two largest Tauna hamlets, Yorampa and Obepimpa, did not even attend. Wepala was still angry at Kawo for trying to marry his daughter and stopped his clan from partaking of Kawo's mumu food. Some of the people were simply weary of Kawo's government lectures and tests of power.

Yet Kawo had to get his irritation across. Addressing no one in particular, he said: "All right, now you have shamed me. You didn't come here when I wanted you to come. This is not a government meeting. This is for my daughter. You are all big heads. Later on I will do the same thing to you!" Sooner or later, his message would eventually circulate to the other hamlets.

Several nights later, I heard the sounds of shrill, unearthly wailing over the heavy patter of rain. It was two in the morning.

"Wo, wo, wo, wo, wooooo. . . . Wo, wo, wo, wooooo . . ." I recognized it to be the sound of a curing ritual. Nenanio, the married woman who lived with her five young children in the next hut, only fifteen feet away, directed it.

Someone was severely ill. I listened outside Nenanio's hut in the drizzling rain and tried to make out the voices but could recognize only hers. The tiny entrance to the hut was completely boarded up with planks. I especially didn't want to be insensitive on this occasion, since I heard only women's voices. I stood and listened outside, as the chanting continued for hours, but I would have to find out in the morning the reason for this curing ritual.

Most Tauna curers were men. Four men in particular were extremely adept at their art. Any adult man, if he felt that he had both the ability and the inclination, could learn to "see" as a curer by eating hallucinogenic tree barks and other plants. Through this supervised training, they would be able to diagnose and cure many daily ailments. Female curers like Nenanio did not have access to pinto, the hallucinogenic tree bark. Their methods consisted mainly of chanting, singing, whistling, and "pulling smoke" from their tobacco pipes.

In the morning, Onka explained to me the reason for the curing. It was to help Tewaka's baby, who was refusing to nurse at the breast. The baby was in ill health. The Awa phrased it by saying that "its skin is loose."

Onka mouthed the standard government explanation: "If she had given birth in the hospital in Okapa, she and the baby would have been all right. But she went into the menstrual hut, just like the ancestors. That is no good."

Kawo or Ila were gone; both had left the hamlet at daylight to hunt for wild pigs. We too left. It was time to take a break from fieldwork.

Our arrival back in Tauna after a week's rest in Goroka was barely noticed. We left and came back to the village without making a ripple. Now, it seemed, we were Taunans, no longer strangers.

Yet some people in the village still avoided me. Many of the married and older women did so, but this was more out of a sense of appropriate cultural conduct rather than fear or hostility. On the other hand, they gravitated to Jackie, smiling and hissing with pleasure when she sat down with them. These Awa ideas of sex roles neatly cut in half the number of my daily relationships.

I especially wanted more contact with some of the older men in the village, like Api. I prodded Ila for days to bring him down from his hut at Yorampa hamlet so that we could talk. I knew that Api, more than anyone else in the village, could help me understand Awa culture and history. All of the younger men, even those as worldly as Ila, saw Api as a man to be respected and treated with the utmost deference. His name was mentioned repeatedly in the stories men told of past intervillage raids.

One dark, windy evening, Api followed Ila back to our house. Api's gnarled hands were clasped behind his waist. In the fashion of many older Awa men he hung a small *bilum* around his neck and down his back. Only women wore these string bags on their foreheads. He stood proudly in the same pair of torn shorts I had seen him with on my first day in Tauna. Api was relatively tall and lean, standing almost five and a half feet tall. But his appearance was deceptive. Great strength seemed to be concentrated in his muscular shoulders and long, sinewy arms. His bald head was marked by a visible groove in his skull, the result of an ax blow he had received from an enemy villager some twenty-five years earlier. His back and legs carried the scars of half a dozen arrow wounds. I could see in his black, steely eyes a man of great intelligence, cunning, and power.

We shook hands in a motion of squeezing them together several times, like working a gasoline pump. Api managed to crack a cautious grin and revealed a betel-stained mouth that was absent of most of its teeth. The three of us sat down on the bamboo floor of my study.

Api spoke slowly and deliberately into the tape recorder. His strong, bony face expressed in great detail the distant memories of war and peace and life and death. Every few minutes, Api asked to hear his narrative played back. The interview was going fine until Api suddenly stopped in midsentence.

"Wait! Wait!" he shouted in Awa. He said something to Ila, and I heard the translation: A sixpence coin, about the size of a dime, had dropped from the torn pocket of his shorts between the warp and woof of the bamboo flooring.

The interview had to be stopped. By candlelight, the three of us fell down on our hands and knees and pulled up the bamboo strips, looking for the lost coin. We spent fifteen minutes crawling in the semi-darkness but could not find it. Api would not forget about the loss of his money.

"Will you repay me?" he asked gruffly. "This is your house and your floor."

I thought about his request for a second and felt that it would have been a bad precedent if I had acceded. I did not want everyone "losing" their money in my house.

"*Awa'mi* — later," I said, using a tactic the Awa regularly employ to put off questions or requests that they do not want to respond to immediately. "Let's continue with the talk about the battle between Tauna and Tawaina. I want to hear the whole story."

When the session was over, I handed Api, with some degree of theatricality, a sixpence "bonus" for being so cooperative. Though worlds apart, I felt that we had shared some kind of understanding. He left the house smiling from ear to ear, clutching the small coin in his pocket.

The drenching afternoon rains became less frequent, and the villagers turned their attention to planting taro, a starchy, underground tuber. Unlike yams and sweet potatoes, taro requires an elaborate irrigation system, especially in the drier parts of the year. Men build these irrigation tubes by attaching long sections of hollow bamboo. They place one end near a stream or waterfall; the other pours downhill into the cleared garden. Most of the time, building irrigation tubes and clearing new garden land was a cooperative venture of kin and friends. Men were responsible for the heavy work of clearing the dense forest, burning down the brush to a stubble, and constructing pig-proof fences. Women did the work of planting the taro tops and, while the garden was growing, the daily weeding and harvesting. For very large gardens (more than 300 square feet), a Big Man, like Api, would mobilize his clan kinsmen and others to clear the garden land all in one day, after which he would organize a *mumu* and kill a domestic pig for their help.

Taro can be steamed in a *mumu*, but Awa women prefer to cook it by first grating it on a foot-long spiny stick. Fresh green banana leaves under the base of the stick collect the pulpy mush. Women spread this mush over more banana leaves, which are laid on the ground in eight- or ten-feet lengths. On top of the pulp, additional delicacies, such as *kumu* greens, edible insects, or cubes of pork, are added. As a final touch, a man will chew up some salt and edible plant leaves and spit this mixture along the whole length of the taro pulp. The long mass of food resembles a giant open-faced submarine sandwich.

Finally, women fold the mush into mature banana leaves, like a giant pole, and shove it into a hollow bamboo tube. They place the tubes directly on to an open fire and cook it until the green bamboo blackens and steams and spits from its own moisture. The pasty mixture cooked

Women grating taro.

Women cooking grated taro in bamboo tubes.

inside the bamboo tubes develops into a hardened grey tubular mass, somewhat like a rubber escalator railing.

We also began work on our garden, a small fifteen- by fifty-foot plot on the north side of the house. We planted no root crops because they were in such abundance in other gardens. Instead, we grew other vegetables. Our best successes were with corn, pumpkins, and squash. Unfortunately, the tomatoes attracted the scrawny chickens around the hamlet. They pecked them right off the vine, leaving them to rot on the ground and attract the nocturnal scavengers. Our final desperate hope was to build a protective cover with a spare mosquito net, supported in four corners with vertical sticks. Soon after, the wind, rain, and sun caused the fine netting to disintegrate; and it turned, quite appropriately, into a rotting burial shroud. Our garden was neither admired aesthetically nor for the choice of foods we grew.

Dry days were good for observing Awa gardening techniques because I could be more ambulatory. One scorching afternoon, I climbed up to the site of one of Api's new taro gardens, which was just being prepared. It lay on a slight slope a few hundred yards away from Yorampa hamlet. By then the Taunans were used to my constant presence and my observations of everything they did. I felt it only fair to lend a hand. I grabbed a spare shovel and started to turn over the dark, rich soil. Not accustomed to seeing me this way, since our own small garden required little spade work, the twenty men and women stopped digging and began laughing loudly, slightly taken aback by this spectacle. Api grinned and wheezed at my unpracticed digging style.

I put the shovel aside and headed toward Api to compliment him on his garden's progress. He still saw me—and always would—as an uninvited guest, but no longer as a physical or moral threat to his way of life. We squeezed hands vigorously. Putting my hands back in my pockets, I grasped a small rubber spider enclosed in cellophane, which had come from a box of breakfast cereal. Without any thought, I pulled it out. I wondered if the Awa would have a name for this object, which was modeled after a dangerous black widow spider.

"What do you call this?" I asked Api.

He looked at it seriously, not looking at me, and turned it over in his palm several times.

"*Gumi*? *Gumi*?" he asked several times, using the Pisin word for rubber. (Api did not speak Pisin, but like most of the villagers knew the Pisin name for foreign-made objects.)

"Yes," I said. "It's just rubber, *gumi*. What is the Awa name . . . ?" Without answering, he grasped it as if it were a delicate treasure and shoved it deep down into his torn pocket to savor it for later.

The menstrual huts in Tauna, usually one to a hamlet, were always quite busy. Once Tewaka left, Ketawa, Ila's fair-skinned younger sister who was distinguished by her blondish hair—I thought it to be a form of albinism—began her occupation as soon as she felt her first labor pains. This was to be her first child, and the delivery was long and slow. The reports from the women indicated that she was in severe pain for hours. We dispatched a young boy up to Kawaina village to inform the local medical assistant that there might be some complications in her delivery. Just at that moment, a medical patrol from Okapa had just arrived; it would be in Tauna the next day.

Two indigenous medical doctors hobbled down the path to Tauna before noon. But by that time, they were too late to help. Ketawa had already given birth to a crying male baby. While she rested in the menstrual hut, the rest of the village had assembled in the *haus kiap* area for a general medical survey. Most of the Tauna people, however, were not very cooperative or enthusiastic, and caring little for any outside patrols. They were all an unwelcome intrusion. One by one, the doctors examined each person. The results of the final survey were startling. About 10 percent of the people suffered from either leprosy or yaws. There was also a 10 percent incidence of visible goiter. Almost everyone had reported occasional bouts of malaria, respiratory ailments, and had suffered from scabies and other skin ailments. The many deep, dark sores made it difficult to distinguish between simple wounds that had been exacerbated from scratching and incipient yaws, a syphilis-like ailment that caused great scars on the skin and the eventual decay of the fleshy parts of the face and hands.

The medical patrol was not well equipped. They had brought only malaria pills, aspirin, gentian violet, and the cure-all, penicillin. Needles were jabbed into bodies for almost every kind of ailment, whether a headache or small cut on the leg. Jackie and I both learned how to load the long hypodermic needles carefully to expel the air bubbles and then to insert the point quickly into the fatty layer above the buttocks. We later had to use this valuable lesson on ourselves.

A day later the medical patrol, wasting no time, left for the next village. The Taunans' attention turned to a special purpose celebration and *mumu*. The reason for this party, according to Ila, was that the children and teenagers were "happy with food." They had earned much money in recent months by selling coffee and carrying cargo and wanted to repay their parents and the older generation by offering a huge, public, intervillage feast, inviting guests and in-laws from Kawaina, Tawaina, and Ilakia, the three nearest villages.

The young, unmarried boys and girls prepared the scene for the five-day-long party of singing, dancing, and eating. On the first day, they sang and danced in front of the *haus kiap* area for a full twenty-four hours, until their throats were sore and they could barely speak. Then they began to decorate the *haus kiap*. The vacant hut where we stayed on our arrival had been completely transformed. Two rows of makeshift tables stood about a foot off the ground. Sheaths of bright green *tanket* leaves hung from the walls and roof. I had the distinct feeling of walking into a trendy Los Angeles restaurant, overdecorated with hanging plants. Each eating place was marked by a large, banana leaf plate. Dozens of bags of rice and tins of mackerel, all bought and carried from Okapa, were cooked in ash-darkened cooking pots. The village elders sat down to eat, ten at a time, and were served a huge spoonful of mushy rice and mackerel. When they finished, another group was led in. Outside the hut, a huge *mumu* hissed with steam.

All the while, the Taunans paraded around in their finest attire. Some of the objects that we discarded months ago appeared mysteriously as colorful body decorations. One aging warrior had wrapped a paper Ace Card Table label around his stomach. Another inserted an inkless ballpoint pen through his nasal septum and wore it as a nosepiece in place of pig's tusks. Young boys decorated their heads with mackerel tins and opossum skins. The bright red mackerel label, depicting a diving fish, could be seen plastered on bows, wooden war shields, and headdresses.

I saw again Ila's air of detachment. If he thought he became indistinguishable from his fellow villagers, some invisible string of shame pulled him back. Ila was the man who couldn't go home again; and there was nowhere else to go. Outside the village in the urban centers of Goroka or Port Moresby he was just another illiterate Highlands tribesman who had come to accept the ways and goods of the Western world. But he had not yet changed enough or seen enough to develop a sense of sorrow about the loss of his traditional culture. To Ila, new was better than old.

The singing and dancing around the flickering bonfires continued long into the night. Some of the more energetic young dancers never rested at all. It was only shortly before dawn that the noisy party began to subside. Only then did the crowing of roosters and snorting of pigs fill the aural void. The first hoarse voice cranked up again at noon.

This was no traditional celebration. My presence had much to do with the timing of the feast and the quality of food. I was a major economic influence as soon as I walked in the village, but the full awareness of this fact only came forth six months later in this fire-lit darkness when the drone of the singing ended, and the villagers went off to sleep, their bellies stuffed with the kind of food that only money could buy.

When four days had passed, I cornered Ila to get him to discuss the events of the celebration in greater detail and to confirm my own observations. We were both in good spirits and well into the proceedings when Mone, a teenage boy from Obepimpa hamlet, tiptoed into the house.

He whispered something in Ila's ear and left quickly. Ila's face showed no sign of surprise.

"The baby of Ketawa, my sister, died a few hours ago," he said calmly. "And so did Kawo's daughter Tewaka's baby, just this evening."

"Oh, I'm sorry," I said helplessly. "What happened?"

"That is the way of babies. Their skins become loose and they get sick and die all the time. . . . Now let me finish the story of the celebration."

The death of newborn infants and young children was so common as to be almost expected; it was perhaps more of a surprise when they survived. Matam, the young father of Ketawa's baby, never even saw the child, since not enough time had passed for it to be brought out in public.

A quiet and hasty dual burial was held the next day in the burial grounds near Obepimpa hamlet. I found its matter-of-factness disquieting. I watched as the bodies of the two cloth-wrapped babies were placed in a shallow round hole and hurriedly covered with spadefuls of dirt. I could hear no crying.

Chapter 6

Empty Talk

The time for taro harvesting and the celebrations and the open-air mumus was over. The season seemed to shift to one of fights and squabbles. Before 1950 and the regular patrols of the *kiaps*, disputes within these autonomous villages were settled by one of the aggrieved participants or an influential Big Man. But now the complaints were handled by the government's village-elected arbitrators: the councillor and committeeman. If they were not successful, the problem would be brought to the court in Okapa and heard in front of the full-time magistrate.

Our presence in the village was important, but not in the sense I thought it would be. Whenever a beating occurred or a fight broke out, the victims often sought us out, not for sympathy or to intervene, but for first aid. After Numia, a newly married of bride of twenty, was beaten by her husband, she came stumbling into our house. Blood from her head wound gushed down her face and neck onto her bare shoulders. But she never cried or showed much emotion. We attempted to patch up the wound by washing it thoroughly and applying bandages. The scalp had been torn, and I could see the skull protruding through her hair and blood. Her explanation was that "[she] didn't do what her husband wanted her to do." Punishing her, the usually mild-mannered Kino ripped a jagged, five-foot-long board from a fence and struck her on the head several times.

Other fights followed during the week; one in Nontorampa hamlet, fifty feet from our house. What started as a playful shoving match between two young boys escalated into a serious fistfight. The ruckus eventually reached the boys' fathers. By that time, the original petty grievances were no longer important. Each father stood silently facing the other, armed with handy, but undrawn, bows. When the insults began to fly, Kawo had heard of the trouble and had come from his garden and interceded in time.

Kawo, however, was having his own daily troubles: his co-wives were not getting along. During our last trip out of the village, he had declared himself married to Aisara, despite the objections of almost everyone. Moreover, he did not participate in the male blood cleansing ceremony before marriage, nor did he make a bridewealth payment to Aisara's father and his clan. These were the two most important conditions that defined a legitimate Awa marriage. Kawo skipped them both and merely acted as if he had married, paying alternating nocturnal visits to Aisara and Tewaka, his first wife.

Whenever the two wives were within thirty feet of each other, they argued and threw insults. The deeper problem was obvious. Kawo favored Aisara and spent much of his time with her. He had given Tewaka little attention since the death of her baby. If Aisara and Tewaka fought, Kawo would often mete out punishment to Tewaka only. After one of these fights, Tewaka limped around painfully, her eyes downcast and puffy. Usually offering us a cheery smile, she became much less effusive. No one could do much about these domestic problems. Marital fights or arguments between co-wives were not considered to be a public issue. The Awa husband was unequivocally the master of his household, and that included his wife or wives.

More than just the co-wives were miserable. Everyone could see growing lines of tension in Kawo's wide, normally smiling face. His own friends and kinsmen thought that he was becoming too authoritarian, too independent, and unwilling to compromise. Kawo needed to do something.

On his way to the monthly council meeting in Okapa, he stopped by our house to pick up our outgoing mail, which we had prepared in a cloth shoulder bag. It was a beautiful day, hot and sunny, with the sky as clear blue as one could see. I felt cheered up by the drier weather.

"When will you be back?" I asked Kawo routinely, handing him the mail pouch. Normally the turnaround was two or three days.

"I don't know," he remarked casually. "Five or six of the other men in the village are going with me to sign up for two-year labor contracts on the coast. We want to make big money, not just coffee money."

"Wh-what?" I stammered out in disbelief. "Who are they? Tell me their names."

"They are some of the men from Yorampa hamlet, Obepimpa hamlet, and Onka and Ila too. We are all going," he admitted.

I was in shock. I was sure that this was the end of my fieldwork. I did not want to argue about their plans or attempt to dissuade them from what they wanted to do. I think I was mainly hurt that I wasn't told their intentions firsthand, especially from Onka, who had chopped the morning firewood as usual, and Ila, with whom I sat and talked for two hours the night before.

I wanted to be alone. I fantasized about relocating to another village or leaving the country entirely. After six months among the Awa, I was broken by the strains of fieldwork and living with a completely different set of rules. Jackie consoled me in my misery. We packed a small picnic lunch of leftover sweet potato and corn and headed up the dirt track in the direction of Tawaina village, hoping that an entirely new visual perspective would change our mood. I shooed the noisy children away; this time they could see that I was serious. But the walk did not help: the pesky insects and the heat relentlessly demanded our attention. We returned to the house after less than an hour and closed the door, trying to shut out any reminder of the village.

My only hope was that Kawo's plan was another instance of empty talk, a common kind of cultural bluff. Kawo himself had publicly stated before that he was against any more men migrating to the coast for work. Fourteen Tauna men were already working there, leaving the village short of available manpower for the heavy gardening tasks. I strained my eyes in the sunlight and saw a half dozen men, distant figures growing smaller and smaller, trudge up the steep footpath to Kawaina village on their way to Okapa. I knew who they were by the color of their shirts and shorts: Kawo, Ila, Onka, and four others. I struggled to control my anger and sorrow.

Sleep came easy, a convenient escape. The following night after going to bed, I heard a familiar voice from outside the bamboo wall.

"Master. Are you up? Are you awake?" Ila asked twice. "We are back. I am not going to work on the coast. Neither is Kawo or Onka or anybody else. We all changed our minds. It was just a thought."

Hearing that news was a relief, but I didn't feel any great sense of elation, and I didn't get up. "Oh, I see," I answered mechanically. "That's fine. I'll see you tomorrow. Good night."

I was emotionally exhausted from having to listen and adjust to all of these contradictory plans, worn down by the children screaming day and night; frustrated from trying to find carriers for the mail and other supplies, and just plain defeated by fieldwork and the unpredictable whims of everyday village life. I closed my eyes and lay my head back on my blanket, and dreamed of a hundred other places where I would rather be.

Onka rushed into the house. "There's someone coming down the Kawaina trail. I think it's John Pokia, the *memba*," he announced.

Earlier, in Goroka, we had met John, a highly personable, articulate South Fore businessman and politician. His constituents of the Okapa District, including the Awa, had voted him in as the *memba*, the representative member for the House of Assembly in Port Moresby. He lived in a large bamboo house on the vehicular road past the rain forest.

John immediately called for a meeting of all the villagers. He was smartly dressed in the style of an affluent local businessman: brown shorts, white shirt, knee socks, and boots. He delivered a serious lecture in mellifluous Pisin. It was the same words that the people had heard many times before.

"If you want money, you have to work. You must build a road from the pine trees in the rain forest to here so that the trucks will be able to come. If you do that, you won't have to break your backs. You won't have to walk so far. You can sell the coffee right here."

Awe, a recent coastal returnee, looked concerned. "But we are not alone," he interjected. "Other villagers—Tawaina, Kawaina, Ilakia, Okasa, Abomatasa—also meet in the forest to sell their coffee. They never show up to do any road work. It is no good if only we Taunans must clear the road."

Other eyes and ears perked up, but John did not respond. "All of you must be at the pine forest in two days. The head *kiap* in Okapa will take a count of the missing persons. If you are not there, you will be fined or sent to jail!"

And that was that.

The interpretation of threat was a fundamental part of the villagers' obedience to the government, that nebulous collective force at Okapa station. Posing next to John with their official authority, Kawo and Ila supported everything he had said. But I had to wonder about their own enthusiasm for the physical labor involved with road building.

Two days later a work crew of thirty men, women, and teenagers—a ragtag band of volunteers laden with shovels and string bags stuffed with sweet potatoes—left for the forest at Kopalupa. One day and night passed quickly. When they returned, they complained that no *kiap* was there to count the people from the other villages that did not show up. Why were they the only ones who had to work?

The Taunans hated road work for another reason: they had to sleep in temporary huts near the Lamari River, a notorious malaria pocket 1,500 feet lower than the village. Several of the workers came back feeling sick and nauseous and lined up in front of the house for doses of Chloraquin. It was hard to tell whether the problem was a malingering effect or the actual onset of malarial symptoms.

Kawo came back well and strong but agitated. "I'll tax every person $3 for their refusal to work on the road!" he threatened. I noticed that I was the only person in hearing distance. I stared at him blankly.

Several days later on a warm Sunday evening, the same work crew, led
by Kawo and Ila, left for road work again. They wanted to be there by
early Monday morning when the *kiap*, it was promised, would be there
for sure. Just before the familiar evening smoke pushed through the *kunai*
grass roofs on Monday evening, Tati, our quiet, muscular neighbor,
returned with a dozen of the others. He plunked himself down
disgustedly on the small wooden stoop in front of his house. I learned
from him what had happened. The Taunans had cleared brush for the
new road all day, but the *kiap* did not appear, nor did any workers from
the surrounding villages. The people's anger at being singled out to work
on the road finally reached the point where they wouldn't do it any more,
no matter who threatened them.

Kawo and Ila were fast becoming the targets of abuse and criticism.
They were accessible. They were Awa. They both lived in Tauna and
represented the village to the District administrators in Okapa. The white
kiaps, on the other hand, who were in complete authority, could not be
challenged directly.

The rest of the work crew walked back the following day. Kawo walked
into the house hesitantly, indirectly. I knew he had something on his
mind, but unlike Ila, he was uncomfortable asking me for favors. A long
pause followed a greeting and some small talk. Then he came straight
to the point.

"Can you write a letter?" he blurted out.

"Of course," I replied.

"I want you to make a list for the head *kiap*. Tell him who is working
on the road and who the bigheads are."

He paused. "And, yes. Tell him I think it would be a good idea to tax
all of those lazy people who won't work. Tell him that I will be in charge
of the tax collection."

Kawo left me to do the typing and headed immediately toward Tawaina
village to threaten them again, this time in person, for not following his
work orders.

A half day later, he returned looking quite pleased with himself. His
glowing smile revealed a large clump of red betel juice.

"I told those bigheads what to do," he said. "If they don't work soon,
the *kiap* will fine them or send them to jail. They have listened to my
talk and they have agreed to work." The few men who were huddled
around our house nodded politely.

Moments later, a teenage boy from Tawaina ran into the hamlet looking
for Kawo. He had come to deliver a message from the village elders. His
announcement was brief: "We changed our minds. We are not going to
work. We are not going to follow your talk. Your talk is nothing. The road
is nothing!" Kawo's frustrated gestures were of no use, and the confused
messenger stalked back toward his village.

I stood there not completely believing what had happened. The problem as I saw it was that no foolproof method of verification could be found to decide what was going to happen and what someone said would happen. I could not yet perceive the differences between lies and truths, actual plans and guileful promises. And it seemed that many of the villagers couldn't either. Were not all cultures built on the assumption that people must share a common system of expectations?

Feelings of vast confusion are unavoidable accompaniments to fieldwork, especially in distant, lonely places where no one can warn you that you are fast approaching the edge of your own cultural reality.

Ila's return from the road work by himself was unexpectedly soon. All of the other coffee sellers had slept down by the river for the night. His now familiar "Good night. Are you up?" cut right through the bamboo wall. I stumbled out of the cot with a flashlight pointed toward the floor and pulled back the door. It must have been two o'clock in the morning. I remembered that Wednesday — payday — had passed.

"Why did you come back so late?" I asked. "You could have waited until tomorrow morning. I'm not going to move, you know."

Ila drew a puff on his cigarette and offered me his usual grin. "Well, I ran out of sweet potato down by the river. There was nothing else left to eat, so I had to come back. Now that I'm here, can I get my pay?"

"I didn't forget," I assured him, handing him a roll of coins. Usually, in addition to the cash I paid Ila, I also gave him cigarettes, twist tobacco, newspaper, salt, and tins of food whenever I thought he had done a good job. That week it was only the coins, and he knew it was because of his frequent absences.

A large part of Ila's attention had been focused on Bokis, his faithful hunting dog, who had been missing for several days. He searched frantically for Bokis during the day and night, in the rain and in sunshine, calling out his name wherever he went. He felt that either a ghost or a snake had killed the dog. He was too upset to concentrate on interviewing work. The loss of Bokis had even curtailed his early morning pig hunts.

Ila carefully fingered the Australian coins. He wanted to prolong our contact. Perhaps he felt guilty.

It was his turn to ask the questions. "Where do these coins come from?" he asked.

I went along with it. "The government makes them from stones in the ground," I replied. "They find them there, and a machine turns them into coins." For some reason this bizarre conversation in the total darkness and growing rain did not seem at all unusual.

"When my ancestors first saw these, they thought that they were ordinary stones — they called them oniki — and threw them away. They were worthless to them," Ila said. "Where can I find these stones?" he asked, under the impression from my answer that the stones were found naturally in places where white people lived. I fumbled for words but couldn't straighten out the misunderstanding and said that I would try to explain it tomorrow.

"Okay, good night," he said. He walked a few steps and added, "Tomorrow Kawo and I will be leaving for the monthly council meeting in Okapa."

Every Thursday was Onka's day off. We collected our drinking and cooking water by lugging it up from the stream in one-gallon plastic containers. Collecting and chopping firewood was more difficult. Usually a clutch of small children — Tesintawa, Kuintawe, Aborate, and Ausi — made a point of observing us prepare the cooking fire. They felt obliged to stand around to see if we made any mistakes or faltered in our task. We did not disappoint them.

I was completely ineffectual at chopping firewood. It was quite disconcerting to have an eight-year-old girl pull the ax from my uncalloused hands and turn a heavy log into foot-long sections in two or three minutes. Next they insisted on starting the cooking fire, but not, of course, with something as convenient as my wooden stick matches. They found some glowing embers in the hearths of their own houses, picked them up with a pair of bamboo tweezers, and blew the red heat on to some bundles of dry grass. Instantly: fire without matches.

Children preparing a fire.

The children always lingered around the house during our dinner time. We usually ate several hours earlier than they did, in the fading evening light; they ate in the darkness and smoke of their own huts. They closely watched Jackie and me as we grasped our forks, stuck them into some fried sweet potatoes, and shoved the bundle of food into our mouths. They gasped and giggled at our every bite. This was a good excuse to ham it up even more. Seeing the intended humor in our exaggerated stabbing motions, they mimicked us perfectly.

Those moments of finding a common humanness in laughter and the absurdity of our taken-for-granted selves highlighted many evenings. The children, it was always the children who showed us and shared with us their uncensored humanity. I desperately needed those lifts. With them I felt that I was just beginning to get a glimmer of what real life in this distant and unfamiliar culture was all about.

During the week, Tenta, one of the migrant laborers who had been working on the coast, returned to Tauna. Tenta was married to Nunuma. He was about twenty-five years old and, at five and a half feet tall, one of the tallest men in the village. His spectacular arm muscles made him look more powerful than most of the other, shorter Awa men. He spoke in a sonorous voice, broken quite frequently by an infectious cackle. A jutting jaw and heavy brow ridges added to his distinctiveness.

Tenta made a spectacular entrance into Nontorampa hamlet, completely disregarding the happy wailing of the older women who grasped at his light brown skin. The contrast of wealth and experience stood out instantly: Tenta was distant and cool and wore the standard shorts and shirt of the returned urban laborer; the older women wore only their musty bark skirts and ratty *bilums* and held back no emotions.

Bedecked in these hard-earned symbols of distant city life, Tenta paraded around like a peacock. He was a worldly coastal returnee, no longer a sheltered, backwoods Highlander. He had seen and done things that none of the women would ever see and the young children could not even yet dream about. Usually, this sense of superiority in the coastal returnees lasted only several weeks until they had to go back to the normal tasks of gardening and regular village life. But it was gravely apparent in some men more than others that a kind of restlessness had infected them. They had been stung by a wanderlust that ordinary existence in the village could no longer contain.

"Where will you sleep?" I asked Tenta, hoping to get an idea of how he would adjust back to Tauna.

"I think," he replied in a slow Pisin drawl, "I'd like to build a house here at Nontorampa hamlet, right next to yours." He gazed outside disdainfully. "That way I won't have to sleep next to all of these backward bush people." He sounded just like Ila.

I was somewhat taken aback. This response of the coastal returnees, which I had heard before, stood out in my mind as one of the more unfortunate consequences of their worldliness. Were they saying that just to impress me, or did they really feel that way?

"I will talk to you later. Maybe I can work for you," Tenta said as he walked out of the house, his large feet weighed down by his thick leather walking boots. I wondered how long it would take him to give up the practice of wearing those boots, a useless gift of Western contact, which were totally impractical in these muddy, slippery mountains.

Ila barged into the house, interrupting my dreamy depression over the outlook of the coastal returnee. "I've found Bokis, my dog!" he uttered breathlessly. "I found him near the garden at Ayantampa. He's dead. I was right. A snake, a death adder bit him on his chest."

Bokis's burial was an elaborate, emotional ceremony. Ila carefully lifted the blanket-covered remains of Bokis, buzzing with dozens of flies, into the shallow round grave next to his house. Many people, some from outside the village, came to chant, moan, and wail over the tiny corpse. Ila wept openly, covering his face and eyes with his hands. The crying lasted throughout the day and night, casting a morbid shadow on everyone around.

A general malaise set in. For days after, I was puzzled by the absence of the younger men around the village. Normally, they were squatting in front of their own huts, relaxing, talking, and smoking. Were they still in mourning?

Tenta, I learned, had returned from the coast with a brand new deck of playing cards. Since the Papua New Guinea Gaming Ordinance of 1965, playing with cards, but not possessing or buying them, was illegal in Papua New Guinea. The colonial government saw card playing and gambling as moral danger, but this did not stop the men on the coast from learning the games that were played on every coastal plantation.

The men played Lucky, a card game fashioned somewhat after European baccarat. Ila and Kawo were part of this regular gambling group, and both were secretive about their activities. They felt, I think, that I would disapprove. Enormous sums of money, as much as U.S. $50 a day, were reported to have been lost. It could take a man months of labor on the coast or selling coffee to save that much. Ila explained to me, however, that these were merely debts owed, to be paid in some indeterminate time in the future. Meanwhile, he convinced me that he needed a daily supply of matchsticks and newspaper as gaming tokens in order to continue playing on a smaller scale.

Kawo boasted that he would eventually use his winnings to pay the late bridewealth for Aisara, the absence of which her father often complained about. Kawo hoped that he could settle the payment for a reduced price, now arguing that Aisara had already born an illegitimate child.

I made plans to talk to Ila about his work experiences on the coast and how he came to learn about cards and gambling and the new magic that the men bought from the Chinese storekeepers who told them that it would help them win. "I'll be there in the morning," Ila assured me.

There was no sign of Ila by early afternoon, and I routinely dismissed his remark as another broken promise. I was even beginning to be used to this. That clearly showed how far I had come in doing fieldwork.

Ausi, the gregarious ten-year-old daughter of Nenanio, our next-door neighbor, happened to stroll by, chomping on a large stick of sugar cane. "Ausi-o," I called out. "Where's Ila? Did you see him this morning?"

She pointed up toward Obepimpa hamlet with her chin and answered in one word: "Lucky."

Ila ambled in to talk later in the day. He was obviously distracted. He eyes focused out in space. He yawned openly and scratched his head.

"I had a headache in the morning and couldn't come earlier," he said, excusing himself. Who was I to believe?

Our lackluster interview fumbled off to a bad start when Onka crept in. He spoke to Ila and me at the same time.

"Tewaka has just returned from her sweet potato garden at Urarampa. She said that on her way back she was surrounded by a group of Auyana men. One of them had an ax and said that he was going to kill her. Then Kawona, the Auyana man who comes to visit her all the time, stepped in. He told the men that they shouldn't kill Tewaka because she was the wife of Kawo, the councillor. But the other men held her until she broke loose and ran back here. She found a group of women to calm her down. She was shaking all over with fear."

Ila jumped to his feet with more emotion and quickness than I had seen since Bokis's burial. "I will organize a meeting at Obepimpa hamlet to decide what should be done about these Auyana men who threaten to kill Tauna women for no reason at all. They should not do this. This is not the time of the ancestors and killing. This is the time of now."

Several of the men at Obepimpa hamlet agreed that they would take turns watching all day and night on the northwest trail toward the Auyana-speaking villages. If any Auyana person appeared, he or she would be fired upon with arrows instantly. The vigilante party planned to keep watch all night.

The following morning I saw Ila looking quite relaxed. He was standing in front of his hut picking pellets of corn from an uneaten cob and was throwing them to his chickens. One of his ubiquitous newspaper cigarettes was tucked behind his ear.

"Ila! What happened?" I shouted anxiously.

He scratched his unshaven cheek and shrugged. "I don't know. I slept all night."

But the matter wasn't over with everyone. Kawo and his teenage cousin on his mother's side, young Mone, left toward the Auyana hills in the morning to search for tracks or any other evidence that might have been there. They came back empty-handed after a full day.

"Did what Tewaka said really happen?" I pressed Ila, trying once again to separate fiction from fact.

Ila whispered, "I think Tewaka was feeling neglected by Kawo because of his attention to his new wife, Aisara. She probably made up this story to get more attention from him."

"Um-m-m," I nodded, beginning to comprehend.

The following cold, dusky evening brought news that Tewaka had been missing all day. Both Kawo and Ila were working in their gardens and didn't hear the gossip in the hamlet. For once I knew something before they did! All during the day, I heard rumors and asked various people what they thought.

"Oh, she's in her taro garden," Tati said.

"She's down by the river," Ayato pointed out to me. Still she was missing, and no one agreed on her whereabouts.

Later in the day, I mentioned these discrepancies to Ila. Almost matter-of-factly, he provided another explanation: "She probably hanged herself from a tree out of shame. She was lying about the Auyana men as I told you, and she is too shamed to come back."

Several days had passed when one afternoon Tewaka appeared at Nontorampa hamlet. She was dressed in her best bright red store-bought skirt and fluffy blouse and walked around as if nothing had happened. She had spent the past few nights with some affinal kinsmen (in-laws) in Tawaina village. Neither Kawo nor Ila seemed to take her absence seriously. I was the only one who seemed to speculate about the "real" reason for her behavior.

Kawo had arranged for some of the other villagers to accompany him back to the other side of the rain forest to do some more road work. The night they left, the voice of Panuma rattled our deep sleep. He had run all the way back in the dark.

"Tewe. Quick. Get up. It's important!" he shouted. Having heard this cry of urgency many times before, I reached slowly for the flashlight and at tortoise-like speed pulled myself out of the cot and stepped outside to talk to him and some of the others.

"There's big trouble at Kopalupa, near the rain forest," he said. Even in the dark I could see he was genuinely agitated.

"Tauna, Tawaina, and Abomatasa villages are arguing over who owns the land and who should be able to use the bamboo and the trees. There's going to be a big fight! Everyone has their bows and arrows ready!"

I didn't quite know how to react to this. I was tired of looking foolish and overreacting to so-called emergencies, and yet I didn't want to be entirely skeptical all the time. I could not travel with the men to Kopalupa. Their normal walking speed was twice as fast as my running speed. It would have been impossible. I softly muttered an innocuous warning to be careful, something that did not translate my confusion very well. Tightly grasping their bows and arrows, Panuma and the other men began their trek toward the edge of the rain forest in the dead of the night.

An unnatural calm hung over the deserted village. The doorways of the bamboo huts were boarded up with wooden planks. The small children and their doting mothers did not seem to be too worried, concentrating on their household and gardening chores. And not all of the men left with the fighting party. Onka, for one, calmly walked into the house in the morning right on time, balancing a plastic jug full of fresh stream water on his shoulder.

"Didn't you go to Kopalupa with the others?" I asked him.

"No," he answered. "I don't like to fight. I would rather work."

"Do you think the fight will really take place? Will any men be hurt?" I pressed.

Onka, reticent as usual, looked at me blankly and wagged his chin. "I don't know anything," he said.

The fading evening light dimly shadowed a party of Tauna men walking briskly down the trail from the east. I strained my eyes to look for signs of trouble or injury but didn't see any. Reaching the hamlet, Ila swung his leg over the low fence and immediately made a turn toward me. The shallow grin on his face showed that things were back to normal. He walked toward me in his usual relaxed posture, his left hand clasping his right forearm behind his back.

"How many enemies did you kill?" I shouted when he was still about twenty feet away.

He approached and smiled. "The big fight did not take place. The Fore people were too scared to fight us. Our Big Men like Api and Entobu wanted to fight, but Kawo and I cooled them down. The Fore turned and left with no argument. We slept there keeping watch and then came back." Ila convinced me that no violent confrontations with the other villages would occur in the near future.

Jackie and I trudged back to Tauna after a week's break, taking the route she had taken the first time. We had to pass through Kawaina village, which sat on the flat crest of a high mountain wall. Resting at the top, I made a 360-degree turn, and all I could see were miles and miles of rolling kunai grassland and the spiny forested backbone of the Highlands. Like hardened bony fingers, the dark green ridges directed the course of rivers, shaped the outline of the forests, and reluctantly offered scattered niches of human habitation. It was easy to see why much of this area had not yet been explored by outsiders since the 1930s and why the Awa had no vehicular road into their village. At the far end of the village, before the footpath descends a thousand feet to the Tauna hamlets, many of the Kawainans had gathered. Their unfamiliar faces were twisted and darkened in mourning.

An important Big Man of Kawaina had just died. Many of his friends and kin for miles around, mainly in the Auyana area, had come to see him buried and speculate on the cause of his death. I was too tired to make any detailed inquiries. Jackie and I looked at each other to pick up our spirits. We shivered in the cold and continued our walk downhill for two more hours until we reached home.

I waited until the next afternoon to climb back up the hill to see what had happened. Women, their faces painted with black or red clay, wailed loudly in the hamlet clearing. The corpse lay on a bamboo stretcher inside a shadowy hut and was covered with several yards of store-bought cloth. The men wore the same material as sarongs. Two somber looking men sat on the ground in a permanent vigil, swatting flies off the corpse with grass handbrooms. The burial could not take place until most of the dead man's friends had arrived.

I was an obvious stranger in the midst of the grief and weeping. My detached voyeurism as an anthropologist disturbed me, and I left Kawaina early, turning down the Kawainan's invitation to talk.

"You shouldn't go walking around all the time," Ila warned me on my return. "A snake just killed one of Waka's pigs today just outside of the hamlet fence. It's a dangerous snake and it kills everything it bites. The air is very bad now for sickness and death. Snakes can smell these things." I listened to Ila's warning and made a silent reminder to myself to always walk with a razor blade and a tourniquet.

When an adult person dies for whatever reason, especially if he was an important man in the village, all of the daily gardening work stops. New plots should not be burned off, and there is supposed to be a general slowdown with everyone's attention paid to the matter of death. Proper Awa mourning means not gardening. Rumors had circulated in Kawaina that Tauna might have been responsible for the death of their Big Man. Malevolent sorcery was suspected. If this was the case, then there might well have been a backlash of physical violence or some other form of revenge. This was only gossip, but it had a real effect: none of the Tauna men would walk up the hill toward Kawaina, especially at night. In fact, contrary to customary expectations, the men avoided the entire death proceedings.

The Tauna villagers had another reason to be preoccupied. Kaye, the eldest son of Api, had just returned from a coastal plantation full of stories, a metal suitcase packed with new clothing, and a pocketful of money. Api decided to sponsor a mumu and kill one of his pigs in Yorampa hamlet.

Kaye, an enterprising and energetic young man of twenty-one, had taught himself to read and write Tok Pisin in his spare time on the copra plantation. He was anxious to replenish his dwindling supply of note paper and pens and headed straight toward our house. We shook hands vigorously.

"How was the coast?" I asked, handing him a new ballpoint pen.

"I had to come back early," he said. "I kept getting fever from malaria and couldn't work. I quit work on the plantation, bought a plane ticket, and came back as soon as I could."

We chatted on the doorstep, and I noticed a huge funnel of gray smoke billowing into the bright, blue sky. It came from the gardens around Wenipa hamlet, in the south part of the village. Kaye saw my puzzlement and remarked, "Oh, that's Ila burning off the trees and brush for a new yam garden."

"But isn't that taboo when someone has just died? Won't some of the people of Kawaina get mad about it?" I asked.

Kaye agreed. "Yes. People are supposed to wait a few weeks, but Ila does what he wants to do."

I did not fully understand the meaning of that remark and made a note to ask Ila about it later that evening. Was he so outside his own culture

Burning off a garden in the distant forest.

that he could do virtually anything he wanted without reproof? Was he beyond gossip and peer pressure? Or was he perhaps a kind of deviant in Awa eyes?

Hours later Ila strolled into the house. I tried to catch him off guard to get a spontaneous answer.

"You said that it was forbidden to burn off the kunai grass for a new garden when a man dies. Now this afternoon you went and did it anyway. I saw the smoke myself. What will the people of Kawaina think of what you just did?"

"I am not like them," Ila said, totally under control. "I don't go around making sorcery against other people. I am the committeeman, a member of the Okapa Local Government Council. Everybody knows that."

Ila's answer didn't help. It just increased my confusion over the apparent lack of fit between what people said and what they did. Every culture has a shared, normative set of expectations to make it function properly, I was taught. What were the Awa rules? Each man, it seemed, acted completely in accordance with his own interests. And some, like Ila, seemed to have much more freedom than others.

Chapter 7

A Rasping Voice in the Night

A message from the South Fore village of Abomatasa had filtered down to Tauna: the Okapa District office was ready to present official government badges to all of the new committeemen in the area. Excited over the news, Ila began his preparation to walk to the station. This meant finding some clean clothes, so that he would look presentable and progressive. Ila did not want to be thought of as a disheveled "garden man," a derogatory term for a villager who cares only for his own subsistence needs.

Ila and Kawo left together. They returned to Tauna later the same day. "The Abomatasa people told us that the meeting was tomorrow, not today," Kawo explained, seeing nothing unusual about the mix-up. I began to see that this consistent style of misinformation did not involve only us! It was more a general kind of ploy, sometimes innocent, sometimes linked to hidden hostility. Ila had the feeling that the South Fore, in revenge for their humiliation at the aborted fight at the rain forest several weeks ago, had deliberately been telling lies to make trouble. "That's their way," he said simply.

Arising before sunrise, Ila, Kawo, Mone, and Tewaka left again for the Okapa station. They anticipated a long stay. Their bulky bilums, which the men wore on their shoulders and Tewaka strung across her forehead, overflowed with leftover, precooked root crops.

Ila stopped by our house on his way up the hill. "First I am going to go back to the South Fore man who sold me one of my pigs. It is no good, it is sick all the time," he complained. "I am going to ask for my money back."

103

"Do you really think he will return it?" I asked pessimistically.

"I will try him out, that's all," Ila replied.

I shook his hand to wish him luck and uttered my usual farewell: "I will stay here. You go."

The following morning, the children's noisy chatter advertised Ila's return. I knew something was wrong. It was too soon. Ila stood before me an hour later, and I prepared myself for what I already knew.

"The South Fore man didn't give me my money back, and there was no meeting in Okapa. They have been sending us this trick talk again." Ila, however, did not seem to be overly upset about having to walk all the way to Okapa and back.

"The real meeting," he preached more confidently, "will be three weeks from today in the Auyana village of Asempa. Master Peter, the head *kiap*, and all the other *kiaps* will be there. I heard it directly from their mouths in Okapa."

The tension from the Kawaina Big Man's death increased in the following days. The Tauna people were afraid to walk through Kawaina to reach the road that winds to Okapa. Instead, they took a long, twisting trail south to the big river and then back east to the rain forest. The gossip was now public that the Kawaina villagers held Tauna responsible for the man's sorcery death. The victim was bitten late in the afternoon in one of his gardens by an extremely potent snake, the death adder. He never gained consciousness. The Kawainans thought that there must have been a more significant reason. It was not an accident. Sorcery was the true explanation, sorcery caused by a man. Why else would the snake have singled this particular victim out?

Kawo and Ila could no longer ignore the loud threats and accusations. The situation had become like a festering boil. They planned to walk up to Kawaina and then to Okapa station to settle the matter once and for all. They first practiced their lecture on me, hoping, I think, to impress me with their strength and conviction.

"You Kawaina bigheads better listen to us because we are going to report you to the number one *kiap*. He will send in policemen with guns and clubs and put an end to all of this trouble." I nodded attentively.

"You can't make sorcery accusations anymore. That is a thing of the past," Kawo continued. "No more trouble!" Satisfied with their recitation, they left for Kawaina. A half-dozen other Tauna men trailed behind, lending them moral and, if needed, physical support. Their handy bows and arrows lay lengthwise on their bare shoulders or behind their necks. The grievance party met with hostility but no real opposition in Kawaina, and they continued unimpeded toward the Okapa station.

The talk they delivered to the head *kiap* must have been persuasive, because the next day two policemen showed up in Kawaina and caused an obvious stir. Each carried a rifle slung over the shoulder. The Kawaina women were sent scurrying off for sweet potato and fresh drinking water. The little children, who had never been to Okapa, clasped their shoulders in awe and fear and were hushed away. The stern-looking policemen repeated in even bolder terms what Ila and Kawo had told them earlier: sorcery accusations were not to be made. Offenders would be sent to jail. Revenge was out of the question. No man could argue against these powerful symbols of government authority and strength.

Shouting early in the morning was usually a harbinger of bad news. Normally only the pigs and the birds could be heard as the valley mist began to burn off. Another man had died.

Kiato, originally from Tauna, moved to Kawaina village several years ago after a fight with his elder brother. Despite his residence in that village, the Taunans always considered him to be "a real Tauna man." The implications were obvious: Tauna saw Kiato's death in Kawaina as Kawaina's revenge.

Kaye, the coastal returnee, was angered that the Kawainans did not call out for him when Kiato died. Kiato was his mother's brother, and, according to Awa custom, Kaye was supposed to receive a death payment in money or goods bought from the store. Kiato was buried in Kawaina after a mumu and small pig distribution to his in-laws and closest friends. No Taunans were recipients of these gifts.

Word from Kawaina passed down from mouth to mouth that the kiap had just arrived in the Auyana-language village of Asempa. It lay in the hills northwest of Tauna nearly a thousand feet higher. A rough feeder road of crushed stone connected it to other Auyana and South Fore villages and eventually to Okapa. The kiap had called out for all of the village committee members to come in person and receive their badges. Hearing this, Ila decisively started out toward Asempa, a walk of two to four hours, depending upon how much he dallied along the way. Tati, our silent neighbor two huts down, accompanied Ila, who carried a half-dozen new bows he wanted to sell to the Auyanans. According to my calendar, I understood the meeting for the committeemen to be next week. Three weeks had not yet passed. But I did not mention this to Ila because I could have been wrong.

Ila returned from Asempa after three days. I had the feeling that the reception for the committeemen did not come off.

"What happened in Asempa? Was it too early?" I asked him.

"Yes. It was too early. Kawaina was sending us lies again. I won't listen to their talk any more."

Two days before the kiap was really due to arrive in Asempa, Ila complained of a stomachache and fever and said that he was too sick to walk. I dropped two malaria pills out of a bottle and handed them to him with a plastic mug of water.

"Take these," I said. "And don't worry about working until you feel better."

The same afternoon, I saw Ila practicing shooting arrows into the stump of a banana tree near his house. Several younger boys perfectly copied his style. Ila held the long, unflighted arrow with his right thumb and forefinger. The bow and the shaft of the arrow were secured by his left hand. Slowly he pulled the bamboo bow string back, releasing the arrow quickly and slightly arching his body toward the target. He was accurate up to about 100 feet away. When his arrow hit the stump of the right tree on target, the boys ran to the tree and rubbed their arrows against the one that hit the mark.

"You look well, Ila-o," I said, obviously hinting to resume work. He grimaced and rubbed his forehead. He had other work to do.

Ila had been making the rounds of the various hamlets collecting money to buy beer at the trade store in Okapa. He and the others wanted to celebrate when he received his committeeman's badge.

On the morning Ila and Kawo were to leave for Asempa village, they decided first to try to settle a dispute that had just developed. Several men from Tauna had beaten up the committeeman from Tawaina village. He was supposed to have secretly caught and eaten an eel from one of Tauna's rivers. The next morning, a Tawaina runner was sent down to inform Tauna to come and collect the fine for this offense. The elderly men around the hamlet sat down and planned their strategy. They agreed that this was a trick. If any of them went up to Tawaina, they would be shot. Several of the Big Men, led by Api, who had not participated in a real fight for a decade, wanted to go up there anyway. Ila stopped them. He said he would go there alone and tell the Tawaina man to come down and pay the fine.

The village was divided on how to settle the matter. An informal court convened outdoors, sixty feet from our house, to discuss the possible solutions in public. About thirty Tauna men showed up. Most of the younger men wanted a government solution. The Big Men—older traditional leaders and fighters—demanded more direct physical punishment. The arguments on both sides began to rise.

Wamani, a bony, underweight Big Man whose stringy shorts hung below his hips, pointed an accusing finger at Ila: "Why do you let Tawaina play around with us? We do not do this to them. You should not even listen to their lies! We are men of Tauna. Why don't you listen to us?"

Ila was not listening.

Wamani grew more furious. He had always set his bamboo-and-twig eel traps in the river where the Tawaina man regularly fished. He argued that the catch was his, or at least should be shared with him.

Ila tried like a polished diplomat to talk to both sides at once. It didn't work. Wamani felt that he was being ignored. Seething with anger, he grabbed his bow and arrows and threatened to shoot Ila. He was serious. He drew back the bow string and aimed the sharp, red-tipped arrow toward Ila's chest. My heart pounded wildly. Forget fieldwork ethics. I could no longer be an impartial observer; I had to do something quickly. The moment I was going to intervene, I didn't actually know how, Api stepped in and lowered Wamani's arrow with his hand. Wamani stormed out of the hamlet in disgust.

"He's just a bighead. Let him go!" Ila yelled, looking unshaken. The court hearing ended for the day.

In the breezeless morning before the sun heated the mud trails, Ila, Kawo, and a half-dozen others set off for Asempa. They returned the following day, this time with apparent success. Ila proudly displayed his long-awaited committeeman's badge on his new, green T-shirt.

Ila's closest friends and clan members decided to hold a mumu at Nontorampa in his honor. Puwate, an older clan brother, donated a small pig. Kawo loosened his bilum from his shoulder and one by one pulled out six bottles of South Pacific Lager. Beer was a precious, expensive commodity to the Awa, and certainly not a high priority item on their shopping list. Kawo handled each one carefully, smoothing his hand on the colorful green label. It had been only since 1962 that alcoholic beverages were available to the indigenes of Papua New Guinea. No longer was it legally only a white man's pleasure.

Kawo set the bottles down carefully on the ground in a straight line, as though they were museum showpieces. Attracted by the bottles, which had now become like sacred totems, the young coastal returnees huddled around and boasted about their earlier drinking experiences in Port Moresby or Rabaul. They talked about the good times they had fighting, throwing up, and passing out. Their rowdy banter excluded all of the women and children.

No men drank at the mumu feast itself. The bottles just sat on the ground, the prestigious symbols of another world. The men waited until dark to drink the beer in the privacy and secrecy of the men's hut, where the bachelors and some married men slept.

The morning was unusually quiet. Ten men, who shared six bottles of beer, lay around Ila's hut recovering from their drunkenness and hangovers. Somewhere Ila had lost his bilum and was searching frantically for it. He concluded that a malicious ghost must have stolen it in the night when he was vulnerable and drunk. Neither he nor Kawo, who sat in a heavy-lidded stupor, was very enthusiastic about walking to Tawaina to collect the fine for illegal eel fishing. Moreover, the possibility of harm had escalated: a Tawaina Big Man had died suddenly the night before. Whenever misfortune, especially death, occurred one after the other in and around these neighboring villages, the devastating gossip of sorcery usually began to make itself heard.

Ila found his missing string bag at the base of a coffee tree near his hut. Nothing was missing, although he was convinced that the ghost did not find what it was looking for. Inside it were a bundle of dried tobacco leaves that he kept in a round tobacco tin, some scraps of newspaper, and a musty passbook from the Bank of New South Wales, Port Moresby branch. I had not known about the passbook and was quite surprised that Ila even possessed one.

He asked me to explain the numbers. I thumbed to the first page and saw two entries: a deposit of $4 in 1964 and a withdrawal of $4 in 1965. He had also accrued ten cents interest.

"You still have ten cents in the bank," I said. I tried to explain the principle of interest.

"When you leave your money in a bank, it grows big, like a tree." That sounded silly and gave the wrong impression. I tried to clarify my point, but Ila interrupted.

"I think then that I will put my money in the bank at Okapa," he said. "I don't want the people here stealing from me."

Compared to the other Tauna people, Ila was a wealthy man. He owned four pigs, often wore new clothing, and his hut, larger than the others, was protected with a plank door and a lock. Inside, his hut was cluttered with store-bought machetes, an ax, spades, several blankets, tin bowls, and a kerosene lamp. His wife, Ruo, owned at least four colorful blouses and many red bead necklaces, also purchased in Okapa. I did not know exactly how much Ila had saved because so much of his money was stuffed away in a battered metal suitcase or entered in the exchange and borrowing circuit, for which men kept only a mental record of debts and assets.

While both Ila and Kawo were stalled over the Tawaina eel dispute, I had my own ideas about court. Looking over our garden, I discovered that a bunch of peanuts I had been admiring for months was missing. There was only an empty hole where it had been yanked out of the ground. Nenanio's children always seemed to know what was going on, so I asked them what had happened.

"Tobi," they said. Our ex-household helper. I called Tobi down from the men's hut.

"It was not me," he protested. "It was Wenamo, the boy who lives in Obepimpa hamlet."

I charged down to Ila's house and demanded that he tax Wenamo for stealing our peanuts. Ila calmly crumbled some dry tobacco leaves on to a small strip of newspaper and asked, "Who planted them?"

"Uh . . . uh . . . Wenamo," I stuttered. Ila lit his cigarette and said nothing else.

Chilly and wet, September scurried in on the trail of numerous illnesses. Everyone seemed to be sick at one time or another. Late one night I awoke hearing a peculiar noise. It sounded like someone or something moaning and breathing like a rasping, asthmatic patient. At first I thought it was one of Nenanio's children wheezing from a cold, but the unnatural sound occurred at such regular intervals that I discounted the idea. The eerie sound, moreover, wasn't coming from any of the adjacent huts. Its source seemed to be around Ila's hut or the stream, 100 feet down a short trail. I listened to it for about an hour and a half until the noise from the rain drowned it out. Ila sat on his front stoop in the morning, drawing in the heat of the morning sun.

"Ila-o," I said. "Last night I heard some strange noises coming from around your hut here. I've never heard anything like it. It was like heavy breathing or moaning. Do you know what it was?" I imitated the unearthly sound.

He turned his concentration to me and his usual placid expression tensed up slightly. "I didn't hear anything like that. The sound you are talking about is that of a ghost who is looking for someone to kill. When a person hears that noise, someone usually dies." I felt uneasy and strange when he said that and did not pursue the matter as I normally would have done.

Poke, a small slightly bow-legged, middle-aged man, came to see me later that day. He wanted some malaria pills. I found that interesting because Poke was said to be one of the best curers in the village, and he almost never sought me out. This time, however, his headache and cough must have been insufferable. Green mucus hung from his nostrils over his sparse moustache, and his puffy cheeks were filled with red spittle and betel. I urged him to swallow the pills on the spot, but Poke, acting as if he knew better, said that "later" would be a better time.

The Awa supplement the Western medicines they receive with their own traditional cures. Rather than being competitive or contradictory, these two belief systems are considered to support one another. In fact, the Awa believed that traditional curing methods improved the efficacy of Western medicines.

Poke chose flashy Konato, another curer, to conduct the curing ceremony. Poke's self-diagnosis was that the ghost of a Kawaina man had shot him with an arrow. He wanted Konato to confirm the cause of the illness. The curing was held in a dark, blocked-up hut, so that no ghost could enter. It was aided by a dozen others who, with Konato, chanted, whistled, and sucked smoke from their foot-long bamboo pipes as a palliative to clear the bad air. Konato shredded *pinto* bark with his fingers and chewed it with a mixture of salt and ginger root. This hallucinogenic tree bark helped him visualize how a sick person's internal spirit essence had been injured and how it could be returned back to the body.

The curing apparently had its intended effect. The following morning, Poke trailed along with Kawo and Ila, who were on their way to Okapa. While they attended a Local Government Council meeting, Poke bought some tins of mackerel and bags of rice to cook for the people who had helped Konato with the chanting.

The reappearance of the sun was cause enough for celebration. Jackie and I strolled up to Wopimpa, a large, cool, and shady bamboo forest several hundred yards away from the house. We desperately needed a change of scenery and a quiet moment together.

We held hands and talked about what countries we would visit after leaving Papua New Guinea, what foods we would eat, and how we would never complain about walking on level ground again. We shared our fantasies about a different life in the future, somewhere else. I had some private thoughts too: why did I bring Jackie here in the first place? I had a compelling reason—to get through graduate school; she did not. Surely the strains of fieldwork in some strange and distant place would be the ultimate test of any relationship.

We followed a small footpath littered with fallen, decaying brown bamboo. Forty-foot tree-like pipes of dark green bamboo rose toward the sky on both sides and dwarfed the smaller shrubs. The thick canopy of leaves at the top allowed only small sprays of light, like dozens of flashlights, to illuminate the ground. Walking through the bamboo forest produced a strange sense of displacement. The usual noises of the village were inaudible. We sat down to rest on a makeshift bench of old bamboo tubes. I crawled around and collected some plant specimens and cleaned off two thin walking sticks that had become part of the forest mulch. After several hours of much needed calm and relaxation, and we headed back to our house.

The moment I stepped over the hamlet fence, the children, who of course knew where we had been, began yelling and pointing. Kuintawe, a bright, attractive, fourteen-year-old girl, rushed toward me and motioned to me to get rid of the plants. I had forgotten that Wopimpa was thought to be one of the most dangerous parts of the village. The people believed it to be the dangerous abode of ghosts and malevolent spirits. Whenever men walked through Wopimpa on their way to and from Tawaina, they did so hurriedly, never resting. One could get seriously ill by merely falling down on the trail or spending too much time in its cool shade. Collecting plants from Wopimpa to bring home was simply out of the question!

Kuintawe yelled for Tati to come out. He scolded me and again described the danger of the situation. I threw my small botanical collection on a slope away from the hamlet and brushed off my hands as I walked back to the house.

When Ila returned, I described in great detail some of the plants I had collected. I asked him to identify them and tell me why they were so feared. One of the most attractive plants resembled a large hibiscus bush, except that it was capped with vivid, open red flowers.

"That one is especially dangerous for the women to touch," Ila explained, "because they will begin to menstruate and eventually bleed to death."

He also told me a story about a *kiap*, who, while on a census patrol several years ago, picked up some of these same red flowers and stuck them in his hatband. By the time he had walked through Wopimpa and arrived at Ilakia village, he was weak and ill with diarrhea and nausea. The last thing I wanted was to be held responsible for the villagers' sicknesses.

Clearly, the growing occurrences of illness and death were not in my control. According to the radio news from Port Moresby, an influenza epidemic was beginning to ravage the Highlands like a forest fire. Beginning somewhere in the Southern Highlands, it was spreading outward to both the Western and Eastern Highlands. The local people had no built-up immunity, and the death toll rose rapidly. Four hundred people had already died.

The radio news from Port Moresby, crackling on our short-wave radio, always began with the grim statistics. The figure reported for deaths the next day topped 500. More than 30 deaths occurred in the Okapa District. I was overwhelmed by fear and helplessness. But nothing that I could say or do, even with my few medical supplies, could prevent something so simple as the flu. During the next week, the toll from the epidemic rose even higher, claiming a total of 1,700 victims to date. I could not tell whether it was my imagination or not, but many more people seemed to be hacking and wheezing and complaining of headaches.

The only balance to the dreadful news was the return of Kuino, another coastal worker. Bearded Kuino lived with Kukawo, his always-smiling young wife, and two small daughters, between our house and Ila's. Like most of the other labor migrants, Kuino suffered from a kind of reverse culture shock for a while. It took time to settle back into village life. A week or more passed before he discarded the walking boots he didn't need anymore and removed his leather cap. The only good thing in the village that migrants seemed to talk about was the plentiful supply of sweet potatoes.

Kuino, who possessed a quick and inquisitive mind, was the only man in the village who owned a portable transistor radio. He brought it to me to examine.

"Maybe the batteries are dead," I said. I slipped them out and fit them in the bottom of my radio.

"Many of the storekeepers trick us," Kuino complained. "They sell us batteries that someone else has used or ones that are completely dead."

It was the batteries, all right. I gave him four brand new ones and set the dial to the ABC in Port Moresby. When he again heard the grating call of a distant world through the static, Kuino's eyes widened, and he shook my hand. He loved to listen to—but did not entirely understand—everything: the daily news in Tok Pisin, the early morning school lessons for Australian children who lived in the outback, late night BBC radio dramas, Western rock, and popular music.

During one early morning broadcast, the Pisin-speaking radio announcer greeted his listeners with a loud "Good morning!" Kuino responded with an echo, "Good morning!" And so it went, Kuino mimicking as much as he could understand of the broadcaster's light-hearted chitchat. I was beginning to miss the sounds of the pigs grunting in the morning. The white plastic radio blaring nonstop out to the world at large from Kuino's house seemed like the worst kind of technological annoyance.

My numbing reflections on the more subtle, devastating forms of culture change were interrupted by another kind of intrusion. A medical patrol from Kainantu trotted down the trail. I could pick out the white shirts and dark boots against the unchanging green background. These were not villagers. The patrol had come to conduct a follow-up study of the flu deaths, which had reached its peak at 2,000. The disease had dissipated, and luckily, no one in Tauna had died.

If anyone still felt ill, whatever their complaint, they were handed aspirin or shot with penicillin. Sotai's wife stepped forward with their two-year-old son, an incurable mentally retarded invalid, hoping that the white man's medicine would be able to help him. The sleepy child and the light of hope in her eyes made me stare down at the ground in absolute helplessness.

There was no smooth transition between wet and dry seasons. By the middle of November the threatening gray clouds offered much more lasting protection to the morning darkness than before, and the hot, dry days became scarcer. A month after the flu epidemic had passed, another medical patrol arrived, this time with something the other patrol did not have—flu vaccine.

Tauna village was one of the last places in the Eastern Highlands to receive the vaccine because it had no road and no cleared level plot of land where a government helicopter could land. No matter. The villagers were ordered to line up for their shots, anyway.

When the patrol finished the circular route around several Awa villages, they called out for some of the Tauna men to cart the heavy medical boxes back up the hill to Kawaina village. Energetic Kaye, who owned no coffee trees and had made no money since returning from the coast, volunteered eagerly. I waved him off, and two hours later he ran into the house nursing a swollen eye and a bloody mouth.

"Kaye-o. What happened?" I asked.

"I fought with the clerk of the medical patrol. What day is today?" he asked abruptly.

"Thursday." He made some small, deliberate marks in his notebook. "What time is it?"

"One o'clock." More scratches.

"Why do you want to know this?" I asked.

"I want to know exactly when the clerk kicked me in the face so that I can take him to court over this. The judge will see my writing and know that I did not lie." Kaye did not explain the reason for the fight.

Later in the evening when Ila and I were discussing some sorcery cases, Konoi, a Big Man of the Aramona clan, walked in and whispered in Ila's ear. He crouched down in a dark corner looking secretive and fearful.

I could barely hear him, and couldn't quite make out the words. I recognized only one. He had mentioned the word *tukapu* several times. This was a deadly type of sorcery that only the South Fore villagers were known to practice. The Awa themselves used other techniques.

"What did Konoi say?" I grilled Ila.

"Konoi says that because of Kaye's fight with the clerk, a South Fore man, the Tauna people are afraid that the clerk might make *tukapu* sorcery against someone here."

Ila then turned to Konoi. "That will not happen. The clerk is not just a bush *kanaka* like the people in Tauna. He has a job in the office. He drives a truck. His brother is a member of the Okapa Local Government Council. He doesn't think about killing and sorcery."

The elderly Konoi nodded, not really believing Ila's answer. Even for other reasons, no one in Tauna wanted Kaye to take the dispute to the courts in Okapa. They knew the South Fore clerk had many friends there. The matter, however, was not forgotten. Word arrived that the *kiap* in Okapa had called out for Kawo to bring Kaye in for a court hearing. The clerk himself had made a complaint.

Kawo stood in front of his hut early the next morning wearing a clean white shirt, to which was pinned his conspicuous councillor's badge. He began shouting in his loudest voice towards Yorampa hamlet, two hills to the east, where Kaye lived.

"Yorampa-ro. Yorampa-rooo. Tell Kaye to get ready to go to Okapa. Hurry up!"

Several minutes later the reply came back. "Nontorampa-rooo. Kaye is sick and too tired to walk. He cannot go to Okapa today. Maybe tomorrow or next week. Nontorampa-rooo."

Like many other disputes and arguments, this one was never resolved. Kaye repeatedly refused to go to the court in Okapa, and Kawo's attention turned to other matters that inevitably arose.

Standing over the valley of Tauna from a distant ridge, I saw a tranquil, untroubled place. All the scars of human conflict, lying, beatings, and death were overshadowed. The beautiful green valley spread far to the south until it was blocked by one mountain wall and then another in a series of undulating waves. The puffy smoke from the swidden gardens of a distant Awa community rose silently and dissipated into the cloudless, blue sky. Seeing such a vast panorama, devoid of any movement, made time seem to stand still.

Jackie and I spent several hours relaxing and daydreaming until the uncooperative insects burst our bubble. We headed back toward the house. Two hundred yards down from where we had been sitting, the footpath was blocked by a large, dead pig. Its four stubby legs stuck straight up in the air, like an upside down coffee table.

It certainly was not there when we first walked up. I took a closer look and could see a slash near the neck. Dimpled bits of white fat and blood oozed out. I told Kawo what I had seen. Hastily, he sent off a half-dozen children to identify the pig. The distinctive black coloring on its back indicated that it belonged to Puwate.

Kawo sent several men to fetch it. They tied the pig's feet to a carrying stick and carried it to Puwate's hut in Obepimpa hamlet, where a *mumu* was already being heated.

Kawo and the other men carefully examined the size, shape, and position of the wound: the verdict was that the pig had been bitten by a ferocious death adder. This probably occurred minutes after we had passed the same spot. Feeling insecure, I tapped the back pocket of my shorts and traced the comforting outline of the handkerchief and razor blade.

Kawo confided in me that to eat a pig that had been killed by a snake was not a good thing to do. He himself had smelled the flesh and said it stunk from the poison in its body. He would not touch it, although many of the others were not so picky.

Kawo came to the house in the evening, not to talk about the *mumu* and the distribution of pork, but about Kaera, the wife of Pauwe. Kaera, a slightly-built woman of forty, was suffering from severe labor pains. We had nothing to offer her except aspirin.

"Don't you have any medicine?" I asked Kawo.

"Men can go down the river and talk to it and ask what they want and then give her the same river water to drink. That's what we do," he said, not showing very much confidence in this method.

Our door rattled in the middle of the night. "Tewe. Do you have any more medicine?" I recognized Kawo's voice.

"For whom?"

"For Kaera, the woman at Yorampa. Her baby was born dead, and she is still in pain."

I gave Kawo some extra aspirin and said, "In the morning I will walk up to Yorampa with you and take a look at her."

Kawo, Ila, and I climbed up the narrow footpath to Yorampa hamlet. I, of course, could not see Kaera in person. She lay in the menstrual hut, off-limits to men. Only women tended to her needs and brought her food and water. Ila suggested to them that she be given a hot drink with sugar and lemon. That would make her expel the afterbirth of the stillborn child.

The Awa believe that a woman can affect her husband's health. Kaera's illness caused Pauwe, her husband, to submit himself to a drastic cleansing and curing ritual. The men from Pauwe's hamlet gathered near the river in the morning. Since polluted blood through sexual intercourse was thought to be the source of much illness, in addition to the ghost of the dead baby, Pauwe needed to have some of his bad blood drained. Washed and naked, he stood in the ice cold river up to his knees. Carefully aiming a small bow and miniature glass-tipped arrow, Entobu shot it into the veins of Pauwe's back, legs, forearms, and, most importantly, the head of his penis. Pauwe flinched back with pain but did not cry out. Blood dripped from his wounds down his clean brown skin into the river, where it could not be collected and used against him in sorcery.

Then the men tied Pauwe to a wooden stretcher, rocking him back and forth over a small bonfire. A wet towel wrapped around his head kept his hair from catching fire. The combined therapeutic effects of heat, smoke, and the draining of blood protected Pauwe from any future illness. A slow ten minutes had passed, and he jumped off the stretcher and bathed his body in the smoke. No longer would the ghost of the dead baby have the power to harm him. The men feasted heartily on one of Pauwe's pigs, which was cooking in a small mumu.

Although Pauwe seemed to be in good spirits, Kaera's health grew worse in the next few days. She became weaker, and her stomach pains did not go away. A group of women from Yorampa sent Ila to fetch Jackie. They specifically requested her.

Ila reminded me, "Don't forget to have her bring the glass."

"What glass?" I asked.

"You know, the glass that you put in people's mouths to help them when they are sick."

The thermometer! The Awa saw it not as a diagnostic tool but as a kind of medicine. Unfortunately, because of the lack of a precise vocabulary, I could not explain its exact function to Ila, and my feelings of ineptitude grew even worse.

Up we climbed for an hour, Jackie, I, and Ila to Yorampa hamlet. Kaera was still secluded in the menstrual hut. Pauwe was in his garden. Even he could not go inside. Ila and I stood outside while Jackie went in, stepping over the small wooden barrier that blocked the entrance to the hut. She carried a thermometer and a vial of penicillin. Later, Jackie told me what she saw: Kaera was comatose and lying on her side on a bed of dried grass. The stench inside was overpowering. Two other women sat inside, doing nothing, saying nothing. Flies swarmed over Kaera's grimy skin. She gave Kaera a shot in the hip. Several minutes later, Jackie crawled back out into the fresh air, holding the spent vial. She knew what she had done was useless.

I urged Ila to carry Kaera to Okapa on a stretcher. "She is weak and will probably die on the way," he said flatly. "We will wait until she is stronger."

The children foresaw Kaera's end and would openly talk about it before the adults.

That night an unusually strong breeze blew from the south, disturbing the pitter-patter of rain. The children looked at me and said it was Kaera's ghost. It had separated from Kaera's mortal body, leaving the filth and excrement and darkness to wander about in a better place.

Chapter 8

Of Snakes and Sorcery

Kawo and Ila did not go to the government's monthly meeting in Okapa alone. Six teenaged boys trailed behind them like sticky shadows. Most of them barely had a trace of a moustache. They insisted on signing up to work on the coast. Migrant fever seemed to hit them every several months. The *kiap* usually rebuffed them, telling them to wait until the other men returned so that the village would not be entirely without males.

This time the boys appeared to be more stubborn and determined. Tia, Ila's younger unmarried brother, returned from Okapa ahead of the others and said that the *kiap* had signed up all the boys. They were to leave in a few days. That surprised me. I knew that some of the people would make it difficult for the boys to go. Most of the women and the Big Men always opposed these plans. They did not want to see their husbands, brothers, or sons leave for two years to a faraway place that they knew little about. Mone was supposed to wait until his older brother, Nonaka, returned, because he was still looking out for his brother's wife. Wenamo was taking care of the wife of Mapika. Complaints about the shortage of help for the heavy gardening tasks also were heard.

Tia, who had heard Ila talk about the coast for years, outlined a plan. The entire village would participate in a cookout on Sunday, after which the six boys would sleep down by the big river. A government truck would pick them up at the edge of the forest on Monday morning, and off they would go to Okapa, Goroka, and then Port Moresby.

Some villagers complained of bad timing. It was only several weeks before Christmas, in the last several years a time of singing, dancing, and

117

intervillage feasts. All of the colonial holidays became indigenous holidays as well, although the meaning and ritual attached to both groups was never the same. As much as I doubted that the boys would actually ever leave, Tia said that the decision was final and certain. He wore one of Ila's new cotton shirts as a going-away present.

Kaye, the recently-returned labor migrant, gloated over the eager, new recruits. He stood comfortably in our doorway. He himself did not want to go back quite yet, but eventually he would. Wisely, he warned the enthusiastic young boys not only of the new sights they would see but also of the unavoidable hardships. They swallowed every word he had to say. Intrigued by the tales of the coast and the exploits of the returnees, these boys hungered for new experiences; nothing could stop them. How could they be kept up on their farms after they'd seen or heard of Port Moresby?

A day later, Kawo and Ila returned from Okapa. Kawo beamed enthusiastically about the last meeting. He called for all the hamlets to come down and hear the news, but no one showed up. He plainly was flustered.

"I will have to tax them for their stubbornness," he threatened.

When Kawo talked about the new laws of the Okapa Local Government Council, he repeatedly used the term *power* in his discussion with me. I had not heard him use that word before.

"The government is one power," he said. "They make laws, and the people must follow them. Now the government has given the power to the councillors and committeemen. This one power has come to me."

Perturbed because the villagers had not even showed up to hear how he had suddenly accumulated power, I changed the subject: "What do you think about the boys signing up for work on the coast?"

"We will wait and see what happens," he said simply.

His delaying remark seemed to mean that he would just let things occur. But I knew by his exterior casualness that this was a sensitive issue, and there would be growing pressure to keep the boys in the village.

This pressure spoiled the plans for Tia's cookout on Sunday. He said that he and his friends would leave anyway.

The drama of the showdown began with the light of day. The sounds of the boys yelling to meet each other at Wenipa hamlet disturbed my early morning sleep. Rising quickly, I saw both Kawo and Ila both looking wide awake, both with new shirts onto which their government badges were pinned. They looked startlingly impressive and capable, as though they had the "one power." I caught up with them just as they headed out of the hamlet. There was already some confusion. Some people said that four of the boys had already left for Okapa the night before. Others thought that they were still sleeping.

Kawo and Ila rushed off to Wenipa, an hour's walk to the south. I did not see Ila until late afternoon. I couldn't wait for the news.

"What happened? What happened?" I shouted, as he approached our house.

"They were all ready to go. They had their clothes and food packed in their *bilums*, but I talked them out of it."

Showing a good sense of theatricality, Ila asked me for some twist tobacco and began to elaborate. "I told them that there were already too many men away from the village. Leaving would be bad for our mothers and fathers. I told them that work on the coast was hard and that some of the masters would beat you for no reason at all and give you very little money for your work and sometimes no food. I told them how lonely it would be away from their kinsmen and clan mates, and how people looked at us Highlanders as if we were like pigs. I gave a strong talk, and they listened to me. I said finally that they could go after the group of men on the coast finishes their work contract. That will be in about eight moons." I don't know why, but I was immensely relieved.

Our discussion turned to the festivities in Okapa during the Christmas holidays. Kawo planned to go to Ilakia village to tell them of the celebration and to talk them into donating a pig or a chicken. Ila was supposed to deliver the same message to Tawaina village. He described the Christmas holidays as "the white man's time for Jesus," and he had his own personal reason for wanting to participate.

First prize in the bow and arrow shooting contest was U.S. $10. The best bowmen from all over the District were expected to compete. Other prizes would be given in the greased-pole-climbing contest, and a singing and dancing competition made up of men and women who were dressed in all the finery and costumes of their precontact culture. Ila admitted that he would only observe the dances and added characteristically, "I am a man of shame. I don't want to be seen in the old-style clothes."

Ila never made it to Tawaina. He got as far as his sweet potato garden when he ran into a man from Tawaina who said that he and several other men were building a store in their village. They made weekly trips to Okapa, stocking up on cases of fish and bags of rice that they then sold to the other villagers.

Ila sped back to his hut and whizzed right past me, barely pausing to say hello. He organized a few of the usual indolent young boys, who were standing around doing nothing, and began to line up post holes in the ground, six feet away from his hut. He carefully marked the position of the postholes, measuring their distance with a length of twine. Off to the side, the perplexed, young boys, working as fast as they could, flattened the fresh, green bamboo tubes for the sidewalls.

"What's going on, Ila?" I asked.

"This is going to be my new store. Now I'll have a business for myself."

I wondered how the heavy cases of fish and rice could be efficiently

Constructing Ila's store.

transported into Tauna and then sold at a reasonable profit. How long would Ila's enthusiasm last?

Ila made progress on his store and worked every evening until he could no longer see. Afterward, we would meet and talk about the day's events in the village. Kawo, Ila informed me, was busy at nightly meetings with several of the curers. They were trying to rid him of his "dream man," who kept haunting him in his sleep. The dream was always the same: all the babies of Tewaka, his wife, would either be born dead or would die in infancy. And now she was pregnant again.

I strolled up to the end of the hamlet to pay Kawo a visit the next morning. I wanted to know more about his disturbing, prophetic dreams and what he would do about them. He stood near his hut tightly grasping a machete. He stared out at the trees and slightly tilted his head, reacting to something that he saw in his head. This inner vision had nothing to do with his dreams. I knew what it was before I asked.

"Kawo, what are you thinking about?"

He puffed up his chest. "I'm going to build a store here right next to my hut. I'll buy fish and meat and rice in Okapa and sell them here."

My doubts about this grass-roots capitalism doubled.

Ila's store was shaping up quite nicely. It was a six-by-eight-foot rectangular shed, made in the same style as their round sleeping huts, except for the swinging door. The walls were flattened and woven bamboo; these were topped by a *kunai* grass roof. A counter inside separated potential customers from Ila. All of the merchandise would be displayed on a wooden shelf on the back wall. It was a perfect miniature copy of the indigenous stores that dotted the road from the rain forest all the way to Goroka.

Ila took a day off from building his store to walk to Tawaina village. He wanted to remind them of the week-long holiday festivities in Okapa.

The Awa had only recently begun to adopt the Western calendrical names of the day, month, and year to mark the passage of time. The former coastal workers, of course, had adjusted to this system, as did Kawo and Ila, who had to know exactly what day to be in Okapa. But life in the village for the other people was different. There was no need to differentiate individual days. Events occurred spontaneously, not on the schedule of some abstract, imported cultural timetable.

We ourselves, who had initially had such trouble with the vagueness of time and planning, began to see little difference in the days, except for the amount of rain and which social activities took place. We tried, however, to observe or at least remember certain holidays, some American and some Australian, hoping to anchor ourselves to the outside world and build up a sense of anticipation. I suppose that we needed to look forward to the future, to know that our birthdays or Thanksgiving or Christmas would eventually come. The Awa needed no such security.

A village singsing.

Starting a few days before Christmas, we threw extra portions of corn and sweet potato to a scrawny chicken that Ila had bought for us. We wanted to fatten it up for a special dinner. On a chilly and rainy Christmas morning, Ila stalked our dinner with his bow and arrow, finally trapping it under our house. We cooked up the stringy, bony bird in a pot with sweet potatoes and shared it with him.

Singing and dancing rehearsals began the day after Christmas in preparation for the big festival in Okapa on the first day of the new year. Every night the unmarried boys and girls danced until two or three in the morning. The men stepped up their search for a wild pig so that they would have meat to share. According to Kawo, only five pigs and a few chickens were promised to be killed in the entire District.

I heard a rumor that John Pokia, the Okapa *memba*, was going to buy a cow to be slaughtered with some of the Local Government Council tax money. Having seen cattle before in the flat pasture land around Goroka, Ila and some of the other men were greatly impressed by their size. Cattle, a relatively new, imported animal that the government had hoped to promote in some ways, assumed the status as a kind of superpig. Ila openly fantasized about someday buying one with the money he would earn from his store.

Meanwhile, Kawo grew more aggravated about the lack of interest the Awa showed in participating in the holiday festivities in Okapa; or maybe it was because he was always being ignored. Following his request, I wrote a letter to the chief clerk of the Okapa Local Government Council saying that Kawo had tried to "mark" pigs from three Awa villages but that the stubborn "bush people" would not sacrifice any to be killed. Kawo finally offered one of his own pigs. He sent Mone to run ahead of the Tauna party into Okapa, request a written response, and then immediately come back. This all seemed very official and proper and, to me, a misguided waste of time.

A noisy rain battered the village on the last day of the year. The slapping fronds of the banana trees bowed with the winds, and even the pigs hid for cover. Only the very old huddled in their smoky huts keeping company with the very young. Everyone else had prepared their costumes and *bilums* and had walked with Ila and Kawo to Okapa. I spent two peaceful but blustery days transcribing a backlog of tapes.

The first group of villagers trickled back late on New Year's Day. Ila stayed at the small hospital in Okapa with Ruo, his wife; and together they sought help for Matime, their year-old, chubby, colicky son. Ila did not even enter the bow and arrow shooting contest. I had a memory of Ila, the doting father, heating up the frigid stream water every morning and then delicately washing his screaming baby in a large painted tin bowl. He even dressed Matime in colorful baby clothes when the other

Ila washing his baby.

children scampered around totally naked. "I learned to take care of babies when I worked for an Australian family on the coast," Ila once crowed.

The *singsing* was a huge success even though the rain drenched everyone. No one from Tauna won any prizes. Kawo, however, sold four bows and ten arrows to the Fore for $9. He used this money to buy a bottle of *buka meri*, dark rum, and a case of tinned mackerel. He and a dozen other men got blind drunk in Okapa.

Kawo, knees wobbling, was in front of the returning pack with a heavy cardboard case of fish on his shoulders. Each case held forty-six individual tins, which sold in Okapa for 20 cents each. Kawo placed each tin carefully on a shelf inside his empty store. The conspicuous picture of the diving mackerel on the red label faced outward, seducing the eye of the buyer.

"How much will a tin be?" I asked them. "Twenty cents," he grunted.

I couldn't quite understand why Kawo would do this. I also could not adequately convey the concepts of profit and cost. Onka had carried back Ila's case of fish and had set it up in Ila's little store. The tins sold quickly. Ila, too, charged only twenty cents a tin. Perhaps trapped by my Western market mentality, I was missing the entire point.

During Ila's absence, I lay ill in bed with chills and a fever from a malaria attack. Jackie kept my strength up with bananas and hot cups of tea three times a day. Kawo stopped by one morning and reassuringly told me that his dream man had said that I would soon recover. But his real reason for stopping by to chat so early was to ask me for some strips of newspaper for rolling cigarettes. I hemmed and hawed a bit before finally giving in. Later that day, I saw several Auyana tribesmen from the north milling outside of Kawo's small store. I walked up there to greet them and peered inside. A few tins of fish were still on display. Sitting at the far end of the shelf was a red and black box of batteries that looked very familiar. I stepped closer and recognized it to be something that I had thrown out a week ago because all the batteries were dead. Piled in a dark corner was a whole stack of newspaper strips, including several torn pages from *The Times* (of London) that I had given Kawo in the morning. I wondered how long he had been selling our garbage and gifts for profit.

The sounds of shouting from Yorampa hamlet scattered all through the valley. Kuino, who was fastening some twine at the end of his bow, cocked his head to the side, straining to hear the message.

It did not sound very good. Tintau and Nabete, a Big Man and his teenage son, had both been bitten by a dangerous death adder during the night. Kuino could not make out how they were or what exactly had happened. He set his bow aside and started up the wiggly path toward Yorampa hamlet.

"Call out for me if they are sick and need some kind of treatment," I said. If they are all right, don't call down at all."

Several hours passed with no word from Yorampa, and I presumed that the snakebite incident had been a minor one. When Onka came in the evening to chop some firewood, I could not tell anything by his permanent, subdued expression. I asked him what he knew.

"They're dead," he said flatly. "They both died in the morning." I listened in shock and disbelief to the rest of the story.

"The snake bit Tintau on the arm while he was sleeping in the men's house. When he felt the snake biting him, he jerked his arm away. The snake landed on his son and bit him too. Api, who was sleeping next to them, heard the noise and lit a torch. He saw the snake crawling out of the men's house and shot it through the head with an arrow."

Ila's younger brother left quickly to summon Ila in Okapa. The two victims were Ila's father-in-law and brother-in-law.

Most of the villagers slept at Yorampa hamlet to mourn and show their respect for Tintau and Nabete. The conversation centered around who or what group of men could be responsible for these deaths of the two men from Aramona clan. Since the victims were so closely related, this surely could not be an accident. Someone must have had a grudge and sent the snake to do its dirty work. The rest of the Aramona clansmen considered moving to another hamlet, perhaps to Nontorampa near Kawo's house, just in case they were future targets of some unknown sorcerer.

Friends and kin of the deceased organized a *kano*, a traditional divination technique used to discover the identity of the responsible party. Pieces of sweet potato collected from different Tauna clans and other villages were cooked in a small *mumu*. After half an hour, the sections of root crops were scrutinized by all those present. The sweet potato that was the least cooked in their eyes pointed to the sorcerer's clan or village. Every day, late in the evening, the *kano* divination took place far away from Yorampa in a secluded area of thicket and trees. Four or five men examined the cooked sweet potato over and over to make sure they were right. *Kano* divination had to be performed many times with the same result to be considered accurate. Sometimes it took several months to discover the true identity of the guilty party. The strains in the village began to build because a week before Tintau had died, he confided to his clansmen that someone had tried to sorcerize him.

Kawo and Ila were noticeably quiet and docile, quite unlike their usual selves. Not only were the deaths sudden and completely unexpected, but trying to discover the cause of them placed a great burden on both men. I kept busy writing letters for some of the men to their clansmen on the coast, reporting in detail the gruesome deaths of Tintau and Nabete. Their dangerous, wandering ghosts were held responsible for sicknesses, lost pigs, and almost any kind of personal misfortune. Nothing like this, so sudden and so devastating, had ever happened in the village in the memory of the oldest people.

I wanted to talk to Api about this incident, since he would be the one to know why it had happened. When I confronted him, he was oddly silent and tried to change the subject. I did not want to pressure him to talk. After half an hour, before he was about to leave, he pointed to one of our wooden traps and said, "I want one of those." He tugged at his decrepit shorts. "The rats have been chewing on them, and I can't sleep at night."

I knew Api was using his weight and power, as Big Men do, to see how far he could get by demanding whatever he wanted. He really did not need the trap at all. I wished, of course, to remain friendly, but I could not afford for him to run over me. I used a delaying tactic.

"I'll give you the traps when we leave Tauna. That will be in about three months."

A proud and arrogant man of the past, Api left the house grinning to himself in satisfaction. I admired his style. As his bald head left my view past the hamlet fence, two of Nenanio's children ran toward me from their hut. "Api is a sorcery man. He is dangerous," they whispered together.

A vague rumor was circulating that Api had something to do with the snakebite deaths of Tintau and Nabete. If the children knew this, then everyone else did also. Yet Api did not seem to be too afraid. He walked everywhere alone.

Accusations always seemed to be expressed indirectly. Proof that Api was responsible would take several more divination sessions, even though he slept in the same men's house with the victims and had shot the snake with his own arrow. Then again, this matter, like so many others I had followed in the past sixteen months, would perhaps never be resolved. By now, I wanted and needed, almost obsessively, to know the final outcomes of the disputes and deaths, not some fuzzy dead ends. The Awa, however, viewed their world much more realistically than me: to them, it was ambiguous and uncertain; it took a long time to comprehend.

Only several weeks later did the villagers begin to return to their normal daily activities. People slept in their own huts and hamlets and tended their gardens more regularly. But the gossip about the deaths did not go away. Fears of more deadly snakes and and further revenge sorcery began to build more and more tension both within and outside the village.

A party of ten Auyana men came to collect their death payments from Tauna. When a Big Man like Tintau died, gifts of money and pork were supposed to be made by the men of his clan to his friends, affines (in-laws), and matrilateral kin. (Death payments for children, women, or young unmarried men were less socially circumscribed, normally only between affinally related clans.) Tintau's clan mates tried to stall the

Burning the spirit out of some snakes.

Auyana by saying that they were poor and owned no pigs or any other significant wealth. They would make good on these payments only when the dozen Tauna men on the coast returned to the village with all their money and goods. So death, like birth and marriage — what social scientists call rites of passage — created lifelong social obligations between clans, obligations that were scored on a mental ledger of balances due and balances paid and could go on forever without ever being settled. Again, a fieldworker's nightmare.

Men from neighboring Awa and Auyana villages came and went from the village. They made a point of visiting our house, looking for something to buy or sell, asking for handouts of tobacco or newspaper, requesting medical treatment, wanting to sing into the tape recorder, or just hanging around and dozing on the floor of my study.

One afternoon, a group of men gathered outside of Kawo's house to discuss Aramona clan's (Tintau's) death obligations. A satisfactory agreement seemed to be reached, and they retired to the inside of the bachelors' hut to smoke and chat. I heard a sudden commotion and laughter.

Tucked inside the bamboo walls of the hut, an Auyana man had found a small bottle of red, oily perfume that belonged to Kaye. I held up the bottle in the light and saw a faded Made in Shanghai label. The men who had worked on the coast knew what it was. The Chinese storekeepers in Port Moresby told some of the gullible Highlanders that this special perfume would attract women to the man who owned it. They charged the incredibly inflated price of $5 a bottle, and they warned the men not to keep it near any places where a lot of women were likely to be. The smell of the perfume was also said to be dangerous to pigs. Everyone had a good laugh on Kaye, but he did not mind. He was sought after for marriage by two eligible young Tauna girls.

That was the only laughter, including my own, that I heard in the village in a month. The many illnesses and deaths in the village persuaded several more men, namely Kawo and Kuino, to learn how to become curers. Since Tintau had died, only three other men were recognized to have this ability to see inside the spirits of others. Ila expressed no interest, saying that he would rather go to the hospital.

Within a week, several more infants in Tauna died from infection or undernourishment. The wandering ghost of Tintau the Big Man could still not be settled or driven to its resting place.

We had been in the village for sixteen months, continuously for the last eight months. The stubborn pounding rain and the unpredictability of Awa life, or my understanding of it, made everything seem dark, chaotic, incomprehensible. It was a good time to leave for one final break. I recorded a superb interview with Api, with whom I had become quite close, only to discover that the batteries in my tape recorder were dead.

Ila (right) greeting a distant villager with a gift of newspaper strips and tobacco.

Added to the terrible misfortunes of the villagers, my persistent inquisitiveness was beginning to seem cold and senseless.

We spent two relaxing weeks in a small cottage in Goroka. Hot running water and electricity seemed like marvelous, mysterious inventions. Jackie and I feasted on as much fresh food as possible in the Bird of Paradise hotel restaurant and then spent several days at Rongo station, with a German missionary couple whom we had met earlier. I looked forward to finishing the last three months of fieldwork. So did Jackie.

We bounced along in the back of a pickup truck toward Okapa, feeling more optimistic than ever before. But in our absence we did not know that, once again, a monumental tragedy had befallen the grieving people of Tauna.

Chapter 9

Cries from the Coast

I saw Kawo, Ila, and ten other Tauna people when the truck pulled into Okapa station. Their faces were long and drawn and gray. They stood outside the single-story, wooden patrol office listening patiently to Dave Bretherton, the new head Australian *kiap*. I lifted my suitcase from the back of the truck when Ila walked toward me. His familiar puckish expression had vanished completely.

"Good day," he greeted me rather distantly.

"What's going on?" I asked nervously.

"Five Tauna men who were working on a coastal plantation near Port Moresby have been murdered," he said point-blank.

Stunned, I vaguely mumbled something. I had read about an incident in the newspapers in Goroka about some plantation murders but had not been able to find out where the dead men were from. Out of all the villages in the Okapa District and the whole of Papua New Guinea, it was hard to believe that this had happened to the people of Tauna. The *Papua New Guinea Post Courier* reported that this was one of the biggest fights in the country in recent years, especially at a plantation. Four of the dead men left wives and young children.

All of the men were killed in a savage bow-and-arrow and ax fight with some Southern Highlands workers from Tari. The Taunans retaliated by killing two of the Tari. An argument had started because a Tauna man felt that he had been shortchanged on his dinner ration of rice by the Tari cook. The Tauna men, working on two-year labor contracts, had only about four or five months left to finish. Several of the wounded were recuperating in a Port Moresby hospital and would have to remain in the city for the long court hearing. We all walked back to Tauna, the last hour in the relentless rain, in total silence.

Back in the village, the grief-filled wailing and mournful singing could be heard above everything else. Dawn and dusk, singly and in groups, every child and adult wept privately and publicly until no more tears could be shed. Their improvised chants told of the deaths of the five coastal workers who gave their lives near the place of salt water, lamenting how far they were from their Highland village that they would never see again.

So soon after the deaths of Kaera, and then Tintau and Nabete, these murders could not have occurred at a worse time. In this small village of 170 people, each of the five dead men was either a brother, an in-law, or a matrilateral kinsman to someone else. Every face and chest was daubed with brown or black mourning paint.

Each morning I heard Ila sobbing alone near the back of his hut for Wanu, his clan brother. Kawo, too, shared the pain as much as anyone else. Kirante, his older brother, would no longer see his wife and four small children.

Five Awa men from Tawaina village were quickly flown home from the plantation outside of Port Moresby because of the fear of further bloodshed. His insides boiling, Api called for direct retribution. He talked

The village in mourning.

of joining forces with men from all over the Okapa District and then walking to Tari in the Southern Highlands, several hundred miles away, for a full-scale surprise attack. All he found was agreement, no real support.

Talk of intervillage death payments and obligations was in the air once again. Visitors from near and far came to sleep in Tauna and wait for their gifts. But no payments were to be made until the rest of the Tauna men returned from the coast and the court hearings. That was to be sometime in the future. Momentarily, the ritual of wailing and crying took priority over everything else. Following Awa custom, the men fired arrows of mourning into a fence near Kawo's hut, crying out the names of the five dead men.

The villagers' throats became hoarse, and they could barely speak in their normal voices. Visitors from the dozen or so closest villages came to join the group wailing. Some of the victims were their in-laws and friends because of intervillage marriages. I felt uncomfortably distant and voyeuristic as I watched these intense displays of emotion. While I shared the grief, I could not be a part of the village experience of it.

Kawo came to the house in the evening and asked if I had any binoculars. "No," I said. "What do you want them for?"

"They showed us some of those looking glasses—binoculars—in Okapa and said that you could see far away with them—a long, long way. I want to see Port Moresby. I want to see my brother's grave."

I tried to explain to him that he would not be able to see that far. He nodded his head and walked away. Twenty feet from our house he burst into a wailing song, crying out his brother's name.

Every day outside visitors came and went. The Tauna women kept themselves occupied by making food for the mumus to feed the guests. There were curing ceremonies at night for those who were ill and thought they had been attacked by ghosts. The bitter cries of bereavement filled all the spaces between these other activities.

Every day many of the male visitors went straight to Ila's hut and then seemed to vanish. I became intensely curious because I did not hear any talking or wailing. I went down to investigate. When I bent over to step inside his dark, airless hut, no one turned around. All the men were totally engrossed in playing cards, gambling with whatever money or possessions they owned. Boxes of matches, cigarettes, some worn-down bars of soap, a few coins, and bamboo combs changed hands every half-minute. Total escapism was the best description of their behavior that I could think of.

If he wasn't playing Lucky, Ila kept busy by discussing and negotiating the amounts of the future death payments to the visitors. My concentration seemed to slip, something I noticed in other people as well. I was not interested in interviewing anyone and did little else than listen to the informal gossip and watch the men play cards. This escapism was deceptive, for underneath the appearance of relaxation and levity much hostility among the men was fomenting. Tempers flared up over any petty disagreement.

Kuino, a normally calm man, and Konoi, Kawo's reclusive father-in-law, began one morning with a shouting contest that started over a broken portion of fence that surrounded the hamlet. In the confrontation, Kuino, twenty years younger than his opponent, slowly drew back his bowstring. Konoi, thin and unshaven, held a sharp machete in his hand, ready to take a lunge at Kuino's chest. It would have taken only a second for Kuino to release the arrow. Kawo and Ila, who were drawn to the scene by the shouting, stepped between the men just in time. The four of them shook from the experience, wondering how and why it had gotten so far out of hand.

Later that afternoon, Kuino was at it again. This time it was with Kukawo, his pregnant wife. The argument started over some coffee beans that she had spilled in the river. I saw him beating her over the head with a grass broom. She was defending herself and striking back at him with a stick. This time, two elderly women in the hamlet broke into the squabble and shamed Kuino with their words.

Trying to beat the regularity of the evening rain, Kawo and Kaye began to cut logs for a *mumu* in Nontorampa. Tewaka, on the night before, had just given birth to a new baby in the menstrual hut. Young Kaye, who seemed to be restless and unsettled since returning from the coast, was spending more time with Kawo, Ila, and me in Nontorampa, and he moved into the men's hut. Compared to some of the others and their petty domestic troubles, Kaye's life was a disaster.

He was supposed to marry Tipia, a buxom, chubby girl of the Obepina clan, who had earlier been "marked" for marriage by one of the murdered plantation workers. But her clan and his clan could not agree on the price of the bridewealth. Kaye was not all that enthusiastic about Tipia. He wryly complained that his "skin would become loose," and he would succumb to some fatal illness if he married her. Kaye gave another excuse: he said that he expected to go back to work on the coast again, sometime soon. Other men in the village agreed that Kaye's hot temper and mercurial temperament had been inherited from Api, his father. Someday, the men said, if he were not killed in Tauna, he would almost certainly be murdered on the coast.

The rumors still circulated that Api and Kaye, father and son, for some unknown motive, might have jointly planned the snakebite deaths of Tintau and Nabete. Kaye grew more protective. Everywhere he went, he saw enemies lurking in the bush. I rarely saw him without his bow and arrows close by his side.

In spite of all the personal conflicts and sorrow, the social effect of which would last for months, the villagers made a conscious attempt to change their mood. The births of several babies began to make this possible. Within the same week, Tatiti, a dark, slender young girl, had just celebrated her first menstrual period. A short period of ritual seclusion marked her menarche, after which time she would be eligible for marriage. Kawo and some of her clan brothers walked to Okapa and bought some fish and rice for her celebration. Her matrilateral kin from Ilakia arrived to join the party.

The wailing for Wanu, one of the coastal workers, grew into full force in Nontorampa, our hamlet. An elderly woman from Wanu's clan, one of his "mothers," discovered in his belongings his bark skirt that he received during his male initiation ceremony. She held the stiff strips of bark in her hands, stared at them, and rubbed them all over her body and face. Tears rolled down her cheeks. Some of the younger children were unable to understand what had happened. They did not know for whom the people were crying or why. They crouched quietly and often threw me a wide grin when they saw that I was watching their mothers and fathers. They had never seen this kind of behavior before.

In the middle of all this commotion, village attention shifted to selling coffee and making enough money to pay for the various death, birth, and marriage obligations. Ila and Kuino organized a coffee-selling party. Being relatively wealthy, at least compared to the moneyless women and children, they did not carry the heavy bags of dried coffee beans themselves. They delegated these tasks to Ila's wife, Kuino's aged mother, and ten young teenage boys and girls.

"*Hariap!* Walk faster!" I heard Kuino shouting, acting like some of the *kiaps* who ordered them around.

The coffee crew returned a day later. Their *bilums* bulged with small bags of rice, tins of mackerel and corned beef, and packages of cellophane-wrapped biscuits. Ila and Kuino led the group, carrying only their umbrellas and knapsacks for their dried tobacco leaves and newspaper.

As if prescheduled, Tewaka made her public exit from the menstrual hut. A cranky, reddish-skinned baby boy, close to Kawo's color, clung to her nipple. Kawo did not want to look at his child just yet, as if glancing at it would somehow jinx its health.

"How has the baby been?" he asked me cautiously. "Has it been crying a lot at night?"

Since the menstrual hut was not far from the back of our house, I could clearly hear the screams of the baby at night.

"Yes, it has been crying," I answered. "Most babies do, you know." Kawo tittered nervously, not fully convinced that his bad dreams were wrong.

Three marriages were in the making, and they helped hide all of the gloom: shy, young Wetape to Onka, our morose household helper; Wenamo, a boisterous teenage boy to So, a woman from Kawaina village; and chubby Tipia to the volatile Kaye. None of these pairings made any sense to me. The couples didn't seem to share what I thought of as compatible personalities, nor did their physical characteristics seem to fit. Wetape, a mere fourteen years old, was almost ten years younger than Onka. So was two inches taller than Wenamo and outweighed him by at least thirty pounds. Bouncy Tipia was unlikely to find lasting marital peace with Kaye.

The first two marriages were certain. The last changed according to the daily whims of Kaye. Special *mumus* were held over a two-week period for the three future brides. Stern-looking clan brothers of the women exerted their last symbolic control over their sisters in a dramatic ceremony near a small river. Bundles of reedy *pitpit* grass were shoved into the brides' nostrils until the blood ran down their tensed chins and necks. Tipia cried out in pain. Clan brothers then rubbed a bundle of spiny, pin-tipped leaves against their sisters' bare backs, making them break out into a crisscross of bloody scratches. Their nasal septums were pierced with thin wing bones of the cassowary. Having been bled and cleaned and prepared by their brothers, the women were now ready to live in their husbands' hamlets.

The late afternoon sun began to drop down toward the highest mountain peaks when Wetape and the procession of her clan sisters from Yorampa hamlet walked down to Nontorampa, passing right outside our house. The hamlet was bathed in a soothing, orange glow. There she was to live with Onka. Younger than most brides, doll-like Wetape stood only four and a half feet tall, and her small, pubescent breasts had just become visible. She clutched a brand new, long-handled shovel in her right hand—a nuptial gift from her clan brothers. A light brown bark skirt completely encircled her waist and covered her upper thighs, indicating her marital status. Shiny pig grease, applied in a thin film, coated her entire body. Black mourning mud for the coastal workers colored her cheeks and gave a painted background to the sliver of a cassowary's wing bone that pierced her nasal septum.

Ila welcomed Wetape to the hamlet and reminded her of her new marital duties: daily gardening, tending to the coffee plants, and washing Onka's clothing. Onka, never seeking to be part of a public spectacle, including his own marriage, did not show up to greet Wetape and his sisters-in-law. Since the bridewealth payment had already been given to Wetape's father and clan brothers, there was no need for him to be excited about the mundane technicalities of marriage. He sat in the dark men's hut, chatting with his friends until his in-laws left.

A young bride of Tauna.

a also refused to take part in the premarital cleansing and bloodletting ceremony. So did Kaye. Both complained that "it would hurt too much." As far as I could tell, there was no strong pressure to make them change their minds. The elderly men and women had in some sense given up; they saw that the past was fading rapidly.

Not surprisingly, both Onka and Kaye were former coastal plantation workers. Seeing the cities and other ways of life their parents could not even imagine, they experienced drastic changes in their attitudes about traditional village life.

Young Wenamo, who had never lived outside of the village, chose to marry So in the traditional Awa manner. Ila and I took the short stroll up to Obepimpa hamlet to see what preparations were made for him. He was still secluded in the men's hut. I stooped over and walked into the hut, seeing Wenamo there alone. In the center of the hut some orange embers were glowing and smoking. All around the hearth, empty mattresses of tree bark or store-bought gray blankets were set on the ground. The bamboo latticework of the inside walls held machetes and *bilums* and several wrinkled pictures torn from our Australian news magazines. A family of four sitting around a dinner table in Sydney, and a thin, attractive Australian woman pointing to a refrigerator smiled at me.

Apart from the magazine ads, the shadowy interior of the men's hut seemed more distant and more ancient than the world of coffee selling, trade stores, and Local Government Councils. But what many observers saw as contradictions in changing Papua New Guinea were not that at all. Very simply, the people were more adaptable and more willing to experiment with innovation than most urban Westerners would ever be.

Wenamo stood up without speaking. He looked completely worn out. He was totally naked except for a curved pig's tusk that ran through his nasal septum and encircled his mouth like a bony mustache. For the past five days and nights, he had been sitting close to the fire in the men's house, where his body was heated in preparation for his marriage. The Big Men told him stories of warfare and sorcery and how he should act toward his wife and his in-laws. That was only the beginning.

Two mornings later Ila casually sauntered into the house and informed me that Wenamo was ready to make his public appearance and leave the men's house. I knew this was going to be the important premarital cleansing ritual that Onka and Kaye had refused. I grabbed my notebook and camera and followed Ila up to Obepimpa hamlet. When we arrived, everyone in the men's hut, including Wenamo and Kawo, were still wailing over the deaths of the coastal workers. The women and children, painted in the black mud of mourning, sat by the low-flamed fires roasting the light brown sweet potatoes in the ashes.

Kawo stepped outside into the warmth of the yellow sunlight, like a master of ceremonies under a spotlight.

"All right! Listen to me!" he shouted. "Everyone come out of your huts and sit down in one place facing the men's hut. Hurry up!"

Slowly, everyone did as he said. And then Kawo disappeared. An hour passed, and I was getting anxious to see how Wenamo, the groom, would make his public appearance.

Kawo suddenly jumped out from behind the men's hut. This time he was dressed in women's clothing — a bright, striped, store-bought blouse, which was too tight around the shoulders, and an ankle-length loose skirt. A newspaper cigarette stuck out from the corner of his mouth. I looked around curiously to see if any other men were dressed this way. I thought that this might be one of those great rituals of transvestism or sex-role reversal that many anthropologists had written about.

All of the assembled women and children kept their eyes on Kawo as he dramatically began washing some dirty clothes in one of Ila's metallic bowls. He called up chubby Tipia to watch him closely and moved her uninitiated hands in a scrubbing motion. Tipia giggled at her inexpertise and covered her mouth.

"This is what you are supposed to do with your husband's clothes," Kawo lectured. "Scrub them good with a brush and some soap. Do it like this."

This was no ancient, arcane ritual of transvestism. It was merely Kawo's attempt, supported by most of the younger married men, to persuade the women to do more domestic work, particularly the laundry. Few of the women themselves owned store-bought clothing, and those who did have a blouse, usually their first purchased possession, did not wear it every day. The idea of washing clothes did not occur to them. It only did to the labor migrants from the coast.

Suddenly, from outside the hamlet, three men leaped over the fence. Kuino, followed by Panuma, was dressed exactly like an Australian *kiap*. They both wore identical battered hats, shoes and socks, clean short-sleeved shirts, and shiny badges, which I could see were borrowed from Kawo and Ila. Ila followed the two into the hamlet, acting deferentially as their local interpreter. He wore his usual Made-in-Hong-Kong shorts and shirt. He set down two large, green banana leaves for Kuino and Panuma to sit on and offered them cigarettes, acting very respectfully.

Kuino and Panuma sat rigidly on the ground, their legs stretched out, and yelled to the crowd of women in Tok Pisin, which, of course, the villagers could not understand. Ila knelt by and translated their every word into Awa.

"Now that we own a lot of clothing, you women must wash these clothes in the river," Kuino announced as authoritatively as a real *kiap*. "Not just with water but with a bowl, a brush, and soap. After that, you must work in the gardens so that there will be plenty of food around. You can't just sit around the way you usually do. That's what backward bush people do. You must take care of the coffee plants so that we can earn a lot of money and buy more goods and clothing. If you don't do this, you will be taxed or sent to jail."

The women pointed and groaned. They laughed at the lengths Kawo and Ila went through to deliver their message and covered their mouths with their hands. Some of them gathered up their string bags and shovels and began to walk toward their gardens, not to obey Kawo's instructions but because they were bored with the same repetitive lesson. Kawo continued his farce, scrubbing clothes and cutting up sweet potatoes, off toward the side. The play wasn't over yet.

Kuino, acting as the *kiap*, asked loudly, "How many young boys want to go to work on the coast?" Two teenagers bolted to their feet and formed a line. They always had to be in a line when they were addressed by the *kiap*. Since they couldn't get enough boys to represent a line, Ila badgered Entobu and Api, the two aging Big Men known to be hostile to the *kiap*, into the line. The idea of them volunteering for coastal work made everyone laugh at the absurdity of the situation.

Voicing a rehearsed speech, one boy stepped forward and said, "We don't really want to go to the coast anymore because five of our brothers have been killed there. The coast is a bad place. We want to stay here in the village and work on our coffee gardens. We can make just as much money, and the work is easier."

Kuino replied in Pisin. "Yes, you are right. And the old men and women in the village should also think about coffee.They should not only think about their pigs and sweet potatoes. That is the way of the past."

By this time, Api and the handful of older men were no longer directing their attention to Kuino or Panuma, the masquerading *kiaps*. The crowd looked off in a completely opposite direction, indifferently puffing smoke from their long bamboo pipes. The men, like the women, began to grow impatient.

A half-hour of the shouting and ordering left only Kuino, Kawo, Ila, and several other younger men translating messages from Tok Pisin to Awa for themselves. Everyone else had gone to their gardens or hid in their huts. A few grunting baby pigs hunted for scraps of sweet potato skin and corncobs.

Wenamo, the groom-to-be, stood leaning against the side of the men's hut, looking puzzled at the entire show. This gathering was supposed to have been for him.

Wenamo's actual coming-out for marriage was delayed indefinitely. I wasn't exactly sure what the men were waiting for. Early one morning, I set out for Obepimpa hamlet and met Kawo on the footpath. He was rushing down to see me so that I could write another letter for him. Wenamo and Puwate, his elder brother, had gotten into a fight over the

Wenamo the groom.

bridewealth payment. Each of them had armed themselves with a bow and arrow and had them strung back ready to shoot.

Rather than running back to the house and writing the letter, I walked back with Kawo to Obepimpa. It took only a few minutes up a muddy trail to reach the huts in the clearing. Wenamo was standing around the men's house with three or four of his teenage friends, still tightly fingering his bow and arrows. Puwate paced around the hamlet pointing and spitting and calling Wenamo "a boy who thought only of copulation." This alleged character defect apparently caused the dispute over the bridewealth. The bride's clansmen were demanding a higher brideprice because of this. Puwate and the other members of his clan did not want to pay any more than the U.S. $80 that was agreed upon.

The turmoil died down in the early afternoon, and Kawo told me that the most important part of the premarital ceremony for the groom, the ritual bloodletting and cleansing, was about to take place.

"There are going to be many, many pigs killed here in Tauna. And men from all the villages around will be coming to see this," Kawo reminded me in his best authoritative voice.

I did not build my hopes up. Living in the village for seventeen months had taught me not to anticipate anything.

I knew something was really going to happen only when I saw Puwate. He rarely left his hamlet, but in the afternoon he walked right past our house and straight down to Ila's hut. As soon as Ila and Puwate started to walk along the trail on the side of the riverbank, I tagged along.

"Where are you going?" I asked Ila.

"It's time for Wenamo to be washed in the river," he answered, not breaking his stride. I had been pestering Ila for a week to let me know in advance when Wenamo would undergo the cleansing ritual. I guess he had just warned me.

A dozen men, none with pigs to kill, gathered around a small, secluded clearing on a riverbank. Ila began to clean Wenamo's mud-and-charcoal blackened body with scoops of water from the river. Wenamo was immobile and did not speak.

Now washed, he stood naked in the ankle-high water, looking as if he was expecting the worst. Konoi, an elder of the Aramona clan, appeared from the surrounding bush holding a small bundle of grassy *pitpit* stalks. While Panuma supported Wenamo's back, Konoi shoved the reedy grass back and forth into his nostrils until they began to bleed. Wenamo's face and the stalks of grass were smeared with his dark blood. Wenamo, as Awa men are taught, did not shout out or scream, unlike the women who underwent this same cleansing. He casually wiped the blood from his face with a leaf and tossed it into the stream.

Wenamo then stepped further towards the middle of the stream. Pinching a pair of bamboo tweezers, he pulled back the foreskin of his penis. Konoi carefully took a razor-sharp sliver of bamboo and deftly made two vertical cuts in his exposed glans penis, on both sides of the urethral opening. Wenamo, still bleeding from his nose and now his penis, plopped back down in the water, letting its coolness soothe his wounds. Now his blood was cleansed, and the sexual contact of marriage would not make him ill.

Kawo left alone for the monthly Local Government Council meeting in Okapa. Ila stayed behind, saying that he would "look after the village." With Kawo gone, gossip spread like a brushfire around the village. Tenta had been having a passionate sexual affair with Aisara, Kawo's second wife. Muscular Tenta, of course, had wanted to marry Aisara himself, but he was on the coast at the time when Kawo proclaimed himself married to her a year earlier.

Tenta was already married to hard-working Nunuma, who was three months pregnant. She and her clan brothers were angry because Tenta had not sent them payments of wild pig or three opossums on her pregnancy. Moreover, he was completely neglecting Nunuma.

The whispering turned into a public debate, forcing Tenta and Aisara to run off together to another village, a day's walk to the north. They did not want to have to face Kawo and the growing criticism at home.

I wondered how Kawo would react. Sometimes he was hot-tempered, but I had never seen him totally out of control. Ila believed that if Kawo had not had the responsibilities of the councillor, both Tenta and Aisara would be shot dead, with arrows through their bellies.

Kawo heard the news of the impetuous runaways from the Kawaina villagers, high on the hill, even before he returned to Tauna. I think he was more upset by the news that Tenta was boasting to be the "boss" of Tauna and was proclaiming that Kawo was "nothing" than he was by the couple themselves. Kawo tried to find some teenage boys to search for Tenta and Aisara, but no one wanted to make the trip. I knew that I would be writing a "Dear Kiap" letter soon.

A bright, pink sunset engulfed the entire evening sky when Kawo appeared outside the house. I lit the stub of a candle and sat down at the typewriter before he could ask me what he wanted. If he walked directly into the house, it was usually to visit. But if he hemmed and hawed outside, it was always more important. I offered him a cigarette to set him at ease.

"Dear Kiap," he began in slow, deliberate Tok Pisin. "The people of the village are bigheads. They won't build roads, dig toilets, or clean their own houses. They always have pigs running around inside the hamlets. I have tried to tell them that this is bad, but they won't change their ways."

He paused and then got straight to the point. "What if a man steals another man's wife? What kind of law do you have about this?"

He ended it: "My name is Kawo, Councillor, Tauna village."

I sealed the letter in an envelope and handed it to him. I didn't know whether he would try to walk to Okapa as soon as he could or whether he would just keep it in his shirt pocket as security.

Several minutes later Ila came in to do some night interviewing and saw Kawo walk up toward his hut. "What did Kawo want?" he asked.

I told him about the letter I had just typed. "Men with two wives always have this kind of trouble," Ila said solemnly.

All the next day Kawo sat in his dark hut thinking. When no one else in Tauna would go to the Auyana country, Nunuma herself decided to go and find out what had happened to Tenta, her husband. I saw her hopping briskly down the trail, her bark skirt swishing with every step. She entered Kawo's hut and sat down. He handed her a newspaper-rolled cigarette (few of the younger women were beginning to smoke this way).

She told him the news: "Tenta and Aisara want to marry each other and live in the Auyana area. They don't want to come back to Tauna. That is all right with me. After I have my baby, I will leave Tenta and find another man." Kawo blew out a ring of smoke, looking like a man deep in thought.

Kawo and Ila and I stretched in the morning sunlight as if we were on cue. We also heard the latest news from the prancing children at the same time: Tenta and Aisara had returned and were sitting in her hut. We all spun around and headed up the short trail. Kawo and Ila arrived a minute before me. Reaching the hamlet fence at Obepimpa I heard shouts of "Fight! Fight!" I stepped onto the tree-stump ladder and climbed over the fence. The fight was already over.

Kawo stood away from everyone, five feet to the side. Ila was standing closer to Tenta. Tenta, whose white T-shirt was spattered with blood, was touching his nose. What had happened in the minute that I had missed was that Kawo, on reaching the hamlet, headed straight for Tenta and punched him in the face. Ila, trying to stop the fight, got hit in the face by Tenta. Both Ila and Tenta were a bloody mess; Kawo was untouched.

Tenta, flailing his bulging, tattooed arms, accused Kawo of making sorcery against him while Tenta was away from the village. Kawo countered by calling Tenta a loudmouth and a "rubbish man," a man of no worth. Entobu, the resident Big Man, persuaded Kawo and Ila to go back to their huts. The fight was over for now, and yet I knew that this was the kind of dispute that could go on for months or even years.

I had hoped that in the last month of fieldwork with the Awa there would be no more fights or deaths or serious problems. The chain reaction, however, had already started.

Chapter 10

Loose Ends

The cold night wind from the south whirred and whistled as if to sing an urgent message. Drifting off to sleep, I thought I could hear in the nocturnal bluster the distant sounds of shouting. It came from somewhere in the direction of Wenipa hamlet, an hour's walk through the forest to the south. Like loud calls at dawn, shouting late at night was not a good sign. I sat up to listen more closely, but I could not make out the words. Nor could I hear anyone else in the hamlet stirring. I laid my head back down and fell asleep.

The bright sunlight of the morning cruelly exposed the bad news of the previous night. While crossing a river on the way to her garden, Kukawo, Kuino's sunny, young, pregnant wife, was bitten on the ankle by a vicious death adder. Shocked and delirious, she had tried to walk back to the huts for help, but it was too late. She spent several hours in an unconscious state and then died at dawn.

Kukawo's limp body was laid on a bamboo stretcher directly in front of Kuino's hut, thirty feet from our front door. Once more the fetid anguish of death and sorrowful wailing filled the air. Kuino broke down at the sight of his young wife's body and fell to his knees. Streams of tears rolled down his face and chest. His two small children, their noses running, sniffled and stared, not really comprehending what had happened.

The rest of the village gathered around Kuino's hut to cry and pay their respects. The mournful sobbing continued throughout the night until daybreak as outside villagers began to arrive.

145

A *mumu* was organized in the hamlet to feed the visitors. This offered a temporary diversion to the unremitting pain of death. While throwing logs on the fire, Konato, the stylish coastal returnee, had bumped into scar-faced Anto, the village "crazy" man. Anto harbored a deep grudge against Konato, who admitted to an open adulterous affair with Anto's wife. We had come full circle. This dispute was raging on when Jackie and I first arrived in the village a year and a half earlier.

Anto felt this shame in public, although most of the villagers felt little sympathy for him. They believed him to be a man who was possessed by a ghost, not really a "true man." He was therefore not responsible for his careless outbursts. (Among other ailments, Anto was possibly epileptic; at any rate, he suffered occasional grand mal seizures.)

Anto stood up squarely, wearing only his red cloth G-string. He had no coastal labor experience, no coffee trees, and no money to buy a pair of shorts. His face was disfigured with burns, which had almost exposed an entire eyeball. He pointed and shouted obscenities at Konato. Konato, a study in contrasts, was dressed in a clean pair of shorts and a cotton leisure shirt. He sat on the ground unfazed, staring at the wild-looking Anto through a pair of plastic sunglasses. Some of the men deliberately began to antagonize Anto, obviously putting on a show for the outside visitors.

Anto could not stand the humiliation any longer. He grabbed an ax and ran straight in the direction where I was sitting on the ground. I ducked. He rushed right past me and began attacking a young boy's bows and arrows, chopping them to bits. Most of the observers thought this sorry, pitiful spectacle was hilarious.

Ila and his younger brother-in-law, Tutu, reached the frenzied Anto and tied his hands behind his back with twine. Ila calmed him down by waving an arrow up and down in front of his face and rubbing ashes on his body. Gently, he flogged him with a soft bundle of *tanket* leaves. Anto gradually quieted down. The visitors continued to find his behavior amusing, and the Taunans made no apology for him.

The vegetables and pork steamed silently in an earth oven in the background. Anto, hands fastened behind his back, wound up again, shouting out to everyone around. One of the Big Men motioned to the crowd to stop talking so that they could hear Anto speak. Anto shouted in a stilted, gruff voice. He accused the men of hiding letters from him that he was supposed to have received from the coast. He could not, of course, read or write. He accused several other men, besides Konato, of committing adultery with his wife. The crowd's laughter drowned out his futile charges.

Anto finally convinced Ila to untie him. He stood up and headed out of the hamlet. Everyone's gaze followed his jerky, unsteady walk up a narrow footpath. A hundred feet away he spun around and ran back. Like a giant bird, he flew into the hamlet holding two long pieces of sugar cane in his hands. He headed straight for the women who were pulling the leaves and dirt covering from the earth oven. His main target was Taiya, his unfaithful wife. He whacked her once over the head until Kaye and Tutu tied him down again. Api, now seriously annoyed at the behavior of his erratic clan brother, ordered the men to remove Anto to a distant hut until the feasting was over.

Not far away, three clan brothers of Kukawo washed and examined her body for signs of sorcery. They squeezed and probed for any unusual blood clots or puncture wounds. Although they found no such evidence, that did not definitely preclude the possibility of sorcery. It could have meant that the sorcerers who sent the deadly snake were more clever and secretive than usual. They would have to use other divination and discovery techniques later on.

Kukawo's body was dressed in a new store-bought blouse and skirt of purple, red, and yellow. This kind and gentle gesture deflected, at least for a moment, the overwhelming ugliness of her death. Her body and face were severely bloated from the snake's venom. Dried, caked blood stuck to her puffy eyes and contorted mouth. A chorus of flies hovered around the areas where her skin had bubbled and split. Fat dripped from her pores. The putrid odor of decay was everywhere.

Api (right) putting corn on an earth oven.

Kaye cut off her fingernails with a bamboo knife and pulled off a ball of her hair to keep as a remembrance. "You people have pictures," he said looking at me. "We Awa have these." Only the gravediggers and I stood at the site of her simple, shallow round grave.

Tenta stormed into the house, and I knew what he had on his mind. "What kind of letter do you want me to write?" I asked him.

"I want you to write a letter to the *kiap* saying that Aisara and I would like to marry each other. I want to tax Kawo and Ila and Panuma for fighting with me and for beating up Aisara."

I hadn't heard anything of Aisara being beaten up. Now I didn't know who or what to believe. I gave Tenta some newspaper, and he walked out of the house in his heavy, deliberate gait.

I decided to pay Ila a visit since I had not seen him for several days. He was ill. He lay on a short bamboo platform inside his hut, covered with an old blanket.

"Ila. How are you feeling?" I asked him.

"I have a headache and some stomach pains," he said, lifting himself up.

"How did that happen?" I expected a supernatural explanation, like the ghost of Kakuwo or one of the coastal workers attacking him in the night, but Ila surprised me again.

"Ruo fed me some beans which weren't cooked right. I'll eat some rice later, and then I will be all right."

"Okay. Come by and see me when you're feeling better," I said. I did not mention anything about work or translating or showing up on time. I had completely lost my taste for the personal confrontation that often goes along with the anthropologist-informant relationship. Ila and I shook hands firmly, and we both knew that each of us had changed.

The evening radio news from Port Moresby confirmed the far-reaching implications of the coastal murders. A general exodus of Highland villagers back to their homes was underway. Not only were Highlanders on the coast fighting amongst themselves, but the recurrent friction between Highlanders and coastal Papuans was also heating up in the cities and plantations.

Two labor migrants from Kawaina village returned to tell the same story. They thought that the rest of the Tauna men would be returning in two weeks. I doubted this, since I knew that most of them were still tied up with the court hearing in Port Moresby. That could go on for months.

In the last few weeks I tried fruitlessly to tie up all the loose ends I had collected: there were numerous unresolved court cases, disputes, accusations and counter-accusations, and unpaid debts and obligations. I supposed I would never know how things turned out.

The tidy tables we anthropologists organize and the concise chapters we write at home are our weak cultural constructions of others' full and eventful lives. But I couldn't imagine myself saying to my committee:

Everything over there was a mess; everything I saw was disorganized and incomprehensible; everything I heard was a half-truth or an evasion. I'm sorry. I really didn't collect any data at all!

The next time I saw Ila, he caught me completely off guard. "Does the white man have ghosts and spirits?" he asked in place of his usual greeting.

I stammered like a dumbfounded informant.

"Ahh . . ." I began to stall. "Some of them do have an idea of spirits and some of them don't. Why do you want to know?"

"The white man has a lot of money. I want to know where they get it from. Do you have this power, this spirit that makes money? Can I buy it from you before you leave?"

Ila looked at me seriously. I had to phrase my answer as precisely as possible.

"Look at the Highlanders, like some of the Fore, who have money. They have gone to the mission or government schools and have jobs around the station."

I named the people Ila knew in Okapa, including a medical assistant, a teacher, and several clerks in the office. I wanted somehow to change Ila's polarized view of the world.

"All white men do not have a lot of money," I continued. His ears perked up. "Some of them are poor in Papua New Guinea and in Australia and in America. They act badly and are what you call rubbish men. They are men of no worth or position. There are many white men like that."

Ila seemed to want to ponder over that last statement. He pulled a half-smoked cigarette from behind his ear and lit it up again. He sat cross-legged on the chair. This chair, a simple aluminum and plastic invention, was clearly a measure of how much some men in the Highlands had changed. Kawo and Ila sat on chairs with their feet touching the floor at the government Council meetings in Okapa. Most of the other young men, never the children or women, made it a point to sit in the chair when they came in the house. All of the elderly Big Men deliberately avoided it. Only once did Api ask to try it. Cautiously, he placed his hands on the armrests and lowered his seat, expecting to stoop down. When that did not happen, he sat straight up, but only for a few seconds, and gave out a big, embarrassed laugh. In all his sixty-odd years, his sturdy body had never been contorted in such an awkward position. Api sprang up and crouched on the floor in a more comfortable position, knees to chest and rear end touching the back of his ankles.

A break in the persistent rain allowed Ila and some of the others to carry a load of their coffee beans to the road near the rain forest. The coffee party returned the next evening, and no one was empty-handed except for Ila, who had managed the whole operation. Everyone lugged back cases of tinned fish, meat, or bags of rice to set them down with a heavy thud in Ila's bare store.

Ila could not wait. He cut open the boxes with deft precision. Struck with the finesse of a great artist, he began arranging the tins of food one by one on a narrow shelf. He took more than two hours getting the symmetry and shape that he wanted.

Kawo walked down from his hut, loping in his usual bowlegged gait, to take a closer look. I could see no jealousy or competition between him and Ila. In fact, since Kawo's store was bare, Ila gave him several tins of mackerel to use as a kind of display. But attention to his store could not hide Kawo's serious personal problems. He looked worn and unclean. He was about to wash himself in the river and then set out for Okapa, where a government literacy program for the councillors was to be discussed.

Ila could have gone but chose instead to tend to his store. He stood inside it and outside it for hours. He gave several tins of mackerel to his mother's clan and to Ruo's clan, but made no sale. He reminded me about some of the machetes and kitchenware that I promised him when we left. He wanted to put these gifts in the store and sell them as soon as possible. I told him that he would have to wait.

Kawo seemed to be a different man when he returned from Okapa. At the meeting, the *kiaps* showed the two dozen District councillors movies of Australia and agreed to starting a literacy program. Most importantly, though, Kawo reported that plans were underway for a road to be built, winding through the high Auyana villages in the north down to the Awa. I nodded politely at Kawo and hoped that he was right. He and Ila and many of the younger men and women wanted a vehicular through the village more than anything else. It would mean easier access to stores and to Okapa station. It would take much less effort to sell coffee, too. There was even talk of pooling money to buy a pickup truck in Goroka that all of the villagers could share. The older villagers were not particularly more enthusiastic about the possibility of more demands on their lives. Anyway, how would the roar and rumble of pickup trucks help them?

Kawo had since accepted the fact that Aisara and Tenta wanted to be together as man and wife. The trouble between him and Tenta ended amicably. Kawo still, however, wanted a second wife. This time he decided that it would be Tomo, the slight, forty-year-old wife of his recently slain older brother. "She will make a good wife," he told me. "She has four children and lots of coffee trees."

Most of the villagers were totally opposed to Kawo's plans to marry Tomo. She was not only ten years older than him; but when Kawo was younger, he used to address her as "mother." Kawo's insistence aggravated the tension between different clan groups within the village. A Big Man complained, "It is too soon for him to think about marriage when his older brother has just died." Tomo didn't seem to care one way or other whether she married Kawo.

One day Kawo was back, and the next day he was organizing a party of villagers to accompany him to Okapa. He promised them that the money belonging to the dead laborers on the coast would be there and that the *kiap* wanted all of the people to show up.

Later that same day Ila and some twenty others returned to Tauna by moonlight. Kawo stayed in Okapa. He was in no hurry to come back. When Ila yawned and scratched his chin early the next morning, I was there.

"What happened in Okapa? Did the money come through?"

"There was no money yet. It will come later." He suppressed a yawn. I knew that the term *later* was very similar to the word for *close*, which they used on my first walk into the village. It could mean anything, from the next day to the next year to perhaps never at all.

I was savoring this analogy of distant time and space when Ila cocked his head to listen to a faraway message. We both walked outside and stood facing the Kawaina hills to the west. A man had just died in the Auyana village of Waipina. Ila was summoned there to collect some death payments of pork and money.

Ila took his time over his breakfast of sweet potato and bananas and then washed his infant son in a large ceramic bowl. Those duties done, he put on his committeeman's badge, grabbed his canvas knapsack and his bows and arrows, and headed toward the steep, forested hills to the north. On the way, he thrashed the bush for wild pigs to make the walk more interesting. He did not know how long he would be gone.

The hamlet lay quiet for an entire day, except for the laughing and screaming of the children and the occasional crow of the roosters. A bright sun baked the ground and made the surrounding mountain forest look more beautiful than ever, like a tropical mirage. The valley where Tauna lay glistened with dozens of shades of green and brown.

I knew the calm would not last. Distant male voices from Yorampa hamlet shattered the peace. I looked up toward the eastern hills and then to Teara, Kuino's aged, toothless mother. She had been spinning between her palms the thin strands of twine that were used for making string bags, but she stopped. She whispered softly to me, out of the range of children: "Someone has died. Someone has died."

No, not again! I couldn't believe it. "Who was it?" I asked. Tell me the name.

Teara mashed her gums together in silence. She would not answer. I laced up my knee-high walking boots and set out for Yorampa hamlet, two mountain ridges away.

I arrived an hour later. All of the villagers who were there stood or sat around passively in separate male and female groups. Api stood off to the side of the men with his arms clasped behind his back. A short bilum hung down his back, and he paced around in the same tattered shorts I saw him with on my first day in Tauna. Although dressed only in these rags, whose original color I could not identify, he carried himself with obvious strength and dignity. He saw me coming in the corner of his eye and turned to greet me. We squeezed hands.

"Who was it? Who has died?" I asked, completely tired of having to ask that question of these people over and over.

"It was Tai. My wife," he answered in a deep croak.

She was Api's only wife at the time, a pleasant woman with a wrinkled belly and a hunched back caused by fifty years of carrying heavy loads of food and firewater on her head.

Because of the suspicion surrounding the snakebite deaths of Tintau and Nabete months before, I knew that eventually there would be a flurry of sorcery accusations and counteraccusations. Api's clan brothers had already established that Tai had been attacked by a sorcerer while she worked in her garden. This was not a natural death.

While Tai lay at rest on a bamboo stretcher, the women began the dirge-like drone and sobbing that everyone had heard too many times before. A full day passed before Ila returned from Waipina and Kawo from Okapa. They walked straight up from Api's hamlet to participate in the mourning, which continued throughout the second and third nights. Tai was finally buried in the burial grounds near Yorampa, one hundred yards from her hut, in the village where she had spent all of her life.

The time had come to leave. We took several days to pack our belongings in small cardboard boxes and suitcases. I made up three separate packages of knickknacks, clothing, tools, kitchenware, food, and leftover nails for Ila, Kawo, and Onka. Other presents went to the men who helped me the most: Api, Tenta, Kaye, and Panuma. Jackie gave gifts of cloth and clothing to some of their wives and daughters and to the women and children of Nontorampa, our hamlet. Too excited to sleep, we lay down on our folding beds for the last time without tuning in to the familiar din of the radio news from Port Moresby, where we would be in less than a week.

The last morning finally came, and Ila tried to track down the carriers for our twenty boxes of cargo. But the people who milled in front of the house were more interested in seeing what we might have left behind. Only ten carriers volunteered to haul our cargo up through the rain forest and then to the grassland to the beginning of the muddy vehicular road.

This was a crisis. Would we be able to leave? There was nothing more I could do, and no amount of pleading would have helped. To emphasize our urgency, Jackie started the long winding walk up the hill before me.

We were really leaving. A half-dozen young girls, always her companions, danced behind, waving and calling out her name. "Sackie-o. Sackie-o. Sackie-oooo . . ."

I still stood near the front of what was now Kawo's house, ten boxes of notes, books, and clothing still scattered at my feet. I didn't expect that either Ila or Kawo would carry them. I looked up and could already see Jackie's bright orange hat a third of the way up the narrow mountain trail. Finally, Ila began to berate the onlookers for their uncooperativeness and managed to collect a few more volunteers, mostly women and young girls.

I steadied the boxes on their shoulders, and at last the caravan of carriers headed out of the hamlet. There will be no sorrowful good-byes, I thought. I shook hands vigorously with Kawo, and then Ila.

"You stay. I will go," I said for the last time. I glanced around, hoping to see old Api, but he was not around.

I grabbed my walking stick and stepped over the hamlet fence. In the corner of my eye I saw Ila standing in the doorway of the house, looking as comfortable as could be, with one arm propped against the side of the opening. Kawo was rummaging through some of our old cardboard boxes.

I shuffled slowly up the hill and did not look back.

Epilogue

All travel is a form of gradual self-extinction.
Shiva Naipaul, *An Unfininshed Journey*

Eleven years later, blanketed by a crisp blue sky, I headed toward Tauna village once again for a brief stay. This time it was much easier; I knew what to expect. Walking through and then beyond the cool rain forest, I caught my breath and surveyed the land before me. The glorious, majestic mountains remained unchallenged, shimmering in the sunlight. The lower elevation grasslands and rain forest had the distinctive smell of musty vegetation, some decaying, some blooming with life. The afternoon air was still and silent except for the cawing of the unseen forest birds whose names I did not know.

No road had yet violated this peaceful grandeur. A thousand feet below me, at the end of a foot-wide trail that darted along the spine of a steep slope, lay the new village of Tauna. Most of the small, separated hamlets of the old village had joined together on the recommendation of the local government and moved to a site alongside a cold, beautiful, rushing river.

I stepped gingerly into the water, trying not to stumble on the rocks that lay on the bottom. Already, many of the villagers, their practiced eyes alerted to the minutest movements on the trail, had formed a welcoming party. Balancing myself in thigh-high water, I looked up for some familiar faces. Perhaps I would see old Api or Kawo or Ila. I wanted desperately to know what had happened to everyone.

I saw Panuma first. A cotton *laplap* hugged his waistline, and a half-smoked cigarette dangled from his lips. That could have been a scene from years ago. He look surprised, almost shocked, until I saw his familiar red-gummed smile and prickly, unshaven face. He pulled my arm and helped me onto the riverbank where a line of about thirty huts began. Dozens of children thronged around me. They stared and pointed openly. I did not recognize any of them. Most of the teenagers seemed to be strangers too. Tall, muscular Tenta approached me, chuckling to himself, and extended his hand toward me.

"Good afternoon, Tewe!" he said in his booming voice.

Tenta had settled down to married life with Aisara, I learned, but was bored with "doing nothing" in the village. Work on the coastal plantations had its appeal, but it was hard and unrewarding. Village life was easier, but it lacked the town's bright lights and diversions. For many of the younger men, both places created an uneasy ambivalence about life.

Instantly, I noticed several changes. The traditional bark skirts that the women wore had all gone. No woman was bare-breasted; an imported modesty seemed to have taken over. The colorful cloth skirts, blouses, and dresses that hung from the ceilings of the trade stores in Okapa where the eyes could not miss them, covered all of them, even the smallest children. Looking deeper, though, the women, like the men, who were still garbed in shorts and shirts, did not seem to be significantly better off. Most of their clothes were ripped and dirty and falling to shreds. And the huts they had built in this new location were smaller and cruder than the ones I had seen before.

The villagers also had built a large, rectangular two-room schoolhouse with open-air windows on the orders of the Okapa Local Government Council. No teacher had ever been sent, and it stood empty and rotting.

Except for Kaye and Kuino, who asked me for some notepads and pens, everyone was still nonliterate. This did not, of course, stop the men from sending messages back and forth to their kinsmen on the coast, where a dozen of the adult men worked. Instead of laboring for hours over each letter, they now sent tape-recorded cassettes back and forth through the mail, receiving them in Okapa. The well-dressed Konato, who had always enjoyed earning money, ran off to the island of Buka with a new young mistress from Tauna. She was one of the first Awa women to have ever been out of the Highlands and on the coast.

The important issues of the day were still the same: coffee growing, local politics, and the road. Coffee planting seemed to have increased, but the money the villagers earned could not keep up with the pace of inflation and the price of goods in the stores. Despite over a decade of pushing for a road to be built with the help of the local government tax money, the Awa still had none. Yet the men still talked and pointed to the hills and forest from where they believed it would eventually wind down toward Tauna.

I gradually caught up on what had happened over the years. Most of the older men I knew had died from various illnesses and accidents: they included Abate, the crafty old councillor from Tawaina; fierce little

Entobu; "crazy" Anto, who had fallen into a fire; Konoi, Wepala, and proud Api, whose shortness of breath and fits of coughing finally overtook him. The women too—the elderly Tiara, toothless Teara, Nunuma (Tenta's first wife), and our two nearest neighbors, Ayato and Nenanio—had succumbed to illnesses or died during or after childbirth.

Onka, our reticent household helper, was still married to tiny Wetape. He was in bad health. A large puffy goiter so bloated up his face and neck that I could barely recognize him. He refused to seek medical treatment outside of the village and had given up on life.

Many of the teenagers, like Tia (Ila's younger brother), Tobi (Kawo's younger brother), Mone, and Toa were now grown men. They all had been to work on the coast at least once in the past decade. Now they had returned, married, and partly settled down. Able to speak Tok Pisin, they talked about wanting to go back to the coastal cities and plantations as soon as possible.

Several murders within the village had created permanent rifts between the clans. Quick-tempered Kaye had killed Tutu by shooting him in the chest with an arrow. The argument developed over the bridewealth payment that Kaye's younger brother was supposed to pay to Tutu's clan. Kaye was eventually arrested, tried in court, and sent to jail in Kainantu township. He escaped several months later and made his way back to Kawaina village, where he now lived.

Kawo had also moved to Kawaina village, which had moved down from its lofty mountain hamlets closer to the big river. When I first saw him, he seemed more disheveled than I had ever remembered him to be. He wore a pair of long cotton pants that were rolled up to mid-calf length. His white buttoned shirt hung over his pants and was torn and turning gray. He offered me his usual hesitant, red-stained smile, and then we sat down to talk. The tragedy was Tewaka, his wife. Angry with her domestic performance, he had one day swung a shovel at her, striking her in the back of the head. She fell and by the next day bled to death. Kawo was trying to raise compensation money to pay to Tewaka's clan before moving back to Tauna. Meanwhile, Tomo, whom he had married amid controversy after his elder brother had been killed on the coast, had also passed away after a long illness. Kawo had remarried, this time to a woman from Kawaina village.

Kawo's time as councillor had expired after three years. In the ensuing time a number of younger men from Tauna and some of the other villages had taken over. But Kawo, as well as many others, were extremely disappointed in them. They didn't attend meetings regularly; they didn't "talk strong" to the local government council for what they wanted; they were weak, ineffectual politicians. When Kawo didn't see the changes he wanted, he refused to pay his annual tax to the government and persuaded others to do the same. In the future, and if his reputation had not been damaged completely, he wanted to run again for village councillor.

I wanted to know what had happened to Ila more than anyone else. Through all the village's struggles, through all the grief and joy, he taught me, albeit on his own time, whatever he could about his people. I did not see him when I crawled onto the riverbank. He could have been working on the coast, or perhaps—I hoped it would not be—he had died.

I walked further on through the village along a narrow trail that led to another smaller cluster of huts and gardens. Ila saw me stumbling along, shadowed by dozens of people, and he ran toward me from his new sweet potato garden. We laughed out loud and hugged each other, not hiding our excitement. Now approaching forty, he still couldn't hide his impishness. He had aged, but he looked well. A touch of gray sparkled in his receding hair. Deeper lines marked his face. (He noticed almost the same things about me.) His bare feet and nailless toes, padded with thick calluses, openly revealed the story of the years of hard mountain and coastal living.

Ila had spent another two years of manual labor on the coast again, chopping coconuts and showing some of the younger Awa first-timers what this different world was all about. I could not share his enthusiasm. The thought of this articulate and sensitive man doing nothing better than hacking away at coconuts and answering "Yessa!" to his bosses filled me with a terrible sense of despair.

Ila's one and only wife, Ruo, was still as graceful and winsome as ever. She stood next to her son, Matime, now a shy and handsome eleven-year-old boy who carried a small bow and arrow wherever he walked. He had been trained well.

Ila puffed on some cigarettes I had brought in and spoke slowly and eloquently into my tape recorder. He said he had a story that he must tell.

> When you were living in Nontorampa, you learned all of the stories of the ancestors. Now when you went back to America and the white man was rousted, the new Papua New Guinea came up. I want to tape this story.
>
> Okay, thank you. My name is Ila. My father's name is Ma. I want this story to go to America where many people can hear it. It is about four villages: Tauna, Tawaina, Kawaina, and Ilakia. They have many worries.
>
> Before independence [from Australia in 1975] the white man looked out for us. That was one way. Now we have changed to a new way, and the black man has come up. I have seen this new way of roads and stores and cattle and businesses and coffee and markets in places like Goroka, Kainantu, Lae, Moresby, and Rabaul. I have seen this way of the new Papua New Guinea.
>
> But the four villages here still have the ways of the ancestors. They think only of gardens, pigs, string bags, and walking around the

mountains. We are like people who died or are sleeping. I want to talk clear about this. Our ways are still the old ways. The law of Papua New Guinea is here, but we do not follow it yet. This is the day of the new Papua New Guinea. It is not the same as before.

I like these new ways. [Kawo interjects: Some people like the new, and some like the old, too.] Yes, the old ways are good, but so is the new.

Now look. There are many children here of the four villages who are just doing nothing. They don't think about school or work. They should go to school and read some books. And then they can go to the big school [the University of Papua New Guinea] in Moresby and learn even more. Then they can look out for their fathers and mothers and the land and take care of the businesses. But they don't do this here. Maybe some teacher can come here?

I want you to send this story to America. They can hear it and think about us. That is what I am asking. That is all.

Before I left, Ila told me that he was going to save his coffee money to buy a plane ticket to America. For some, the road from Awa had stretched farther than ever before.

The vast, damp forest of pine trees began to dwindle and take a different shape as workers from a distant sawmill cut into its fringes. Almost twenty years later to the day I first walked through there, I received a letter at home in hand-scrawled Pisin. It was the letter I dreaded. Ila had died. *Would I hurry and come and stand by his grave?* Ila was buried near the foot of the high forest, where the road was going to be.

Glossary

ARAMONA. A clan group of Tauna village.

ASEMPA. An Auyana-language village.

AUYANA. A related language group north of the Awa.

AWA. A language group of 1,500 speakers residing in the southern part of the Eastern Highlands Province.

BIG MAN. A traditional political leader of a clan or village.

BILUM. A traditional woven string bag worn by both sexes and used for carrying food or other possessions.

BUS KANAKA. A derogatory term for an unsophisticated rural villager.

FORE. A language group to the west and north of the Awa; they are sometimes referred to more specifically as the North Fore and South Fore.

GOROKA. An urban area and provincial capital of the Eastern Highlands.

HAUS KIAP. A hut in each village reserved for census and medical patrols.

ILAKIA. An Awa village south of Tauna.

ILASA. A Fore village south of Tauna.

KAINANTU. A small township in the Eastern Highlands, north of the Awa.

KANAKA. An indigene; see also *Bus kanaka*.

KANDERE. A relative on one's mother's side.

KANO. An Awa divination technique of examining cooked sweet potatoes to discover the identity of a sorcerer.

KAPUL. An opossum or tree kangaroo.

KAWAINA. An Auyana-language village west and uphill from Tauna.

KIAP. A (usually Australian) government patrol officer, as the term was used before independence in 1975.

KOPALUPA. An area of grassland marking the border between the Awa and South Fore.

KUMU. An edible spinach-like vegetable (Aibika or Amaranth).

KUNAI. A waist-high grass used as roofing material; the grasslands.

LAPLAP. A wraparound cloth skirt or sarong.

LONGLONG. Crazy, demented.

MEMBA. Member of the government House of Assembly in Port Moresby.

MOBUTAH. An Awa village south of Tauna.

MUMU. An outdoor earth-oven and cookout.

NONTORAMPA. A Tauna hamlet.

OBEPIMPA. A Tauna hamlet.

OBEPINA. A clan group of Tauna village.

OGARATAPA. An Awa village east of Tauna.

OKAPA. The government District office or station.

OKASA. A South Fore village.

PINTO. A hallucinogenic tree bark (*Galbulimima belgraveana*) eaten during Awa curing ceremonies.

PISIN. See *Tok Pisin*.

PITPIT. An asparagus-like edible plant or its grassy stem (Highland *pitpit*: *Setaria palmifolia*; Lowland *pitpit*: *Sacharum edule*).

PORT MORESBY. The administrative capital of Papua New Guinea on the south coast.

SINGSING. A festival of group singing and dancing.

TAMBU. Something that is taboo or forbidden; or an affine (in-law), a relative by marriage.

TANKET. Decorative leaves (*Taetsia fructicosa*) often used to cover the lower body as clothing.

TAUNA. An Awa-language village of 170 people in the Eastern Highlands.

TAWAINA. An Awa village east of Tauna.

TOK PISIN. The most commonly shared language of Papua New Guinea; the lingua franca used among 700 or more indigenous language groups.

TUKAPU. A type of deadly sorcery or murder practiced mainly by the Fore.

YORAMPA. A Tauna hamlet.

WENIPA. A Tauna hamlet.

Suggested Readings

Amarshi, Azeem, Kenneth Good, and Rex Mortimer. (1979). *Development and dependency: The political economy of Papua New Guinea.* Melbourne: Oxford University Press.

Boyd, David. (1981). Village agriculture and labor migration: Interrelated production activities among the Ilakia Awa of Papua New Guinea. *American Ethnologist, 8*(1), 74-93.

Clifford, James and George Marcus (Eds.). (1986). *Writing culture.* Berkeley: University of California Press.

Conroy, John D. (1982). *Essays on the development experience in Papua New Guinea. IASER Monograph 17.* Boroko, Papua New Guinea: IASER.

Grossman, Lawrence. (1984). *Peasants, subsistence ecology and development in the Highlands of Papua New Guinea.* Princeton, NJ: Princeton University Press.

Hayano, David M. (1973a). Sorcery death, proximity, and the perception of out-groups: The Tauna Awa of New Guinea. *Ethnology, 12*(2), 179-91.

_____. (1973b). Individual correlates of coffee adoption in the New Guinea Highlands. *Human Organization, 32*(3), 305-14.

_____. (1974a). Marriage, alliance, and warfare: A view from the New Guinea Highlands. *American Ethnologist, 1*(2), 281-93.

_____. (1974b). Misfortune and traditional political leadership among the Tauna Awa of New Guinea. *Oceania, 45*(1), 18-26.

_____. (1975). Character control and the message of mediums. *Mankind, 10,* 99-104.

_____. (1978). Cognitive footprints from the past: Clues to the settlement of a New Guinea village. *Mankind, 11,* 461-67.

_____. (1979). Male migrant labour and changing sex roles in a Papua New Guinea Highlands society. *Oceania, 50*(1), 37-52.

_____. (1982). Models for alcohol use and drunkenness among the Awa, Eastern Highlands. In Mac Marshall (Ed.), *Through a glass darkly: Beer and Modernization in Papua New Guinea,* (pp. 217-26). Boroko, Papua New Guinea: IASER.

_____. (1989). Like eating money: Card gambling in a Papua New Guinea Highlands village. *Journal of Gambling Behavior, 5*(3), 231-45.

Langness, L. L., and Terence Hays. (Eds.) (1987). *Anthropology in the High Valleys.* Novato, CA: Chandler and Sharp.

Marcus, George, and Michael Fischer. (1986). *Anthropology as cultural critique.* Chicago: University of Chicago Press.

Mitchell, William. (1987). *The bamboo fire: Field work with the New Guinea Wape* (2nd ed.). Prospect Heights, Ill.: Waveland Press.

Nelson, Hank. (1982). *Taim Bilong Masta.* Sydney: Australian Broadcasting Commission.

Newman, Philip, and David Boyd. (1982). The making of men: Ritual and meaning in Awa male initiation. In Gilbert H. Herdt (Ed.), *Rituals of manhood: Male initiation in Papua New Guinea,* (pp. 239-85). Berkeley: University of California Press.

Pataki-Schweizer, K. J. (1980). *A New Guinea landscape.* Seattle: University of Washington Press.

Read, Kenneth. (1965). *The high valley.* New York: Scribner's.

_____. (1986). *Return to the high valley.* Berkeley: University of California Press.

Rosaldo, Renato. (1989). *Culture and truth: The remaking of social analysis.* Boston: Beacon Press.

Ross, Anthony. (1984). *Migrants from fifty villages. IASER Monograph 21.* Boroko, Papua New Guinea: IASER.

Sinclair, James. (1981). *Kiap.* Sydney: Pacific Publications.